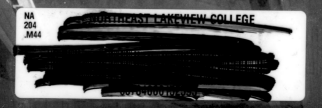

...isms

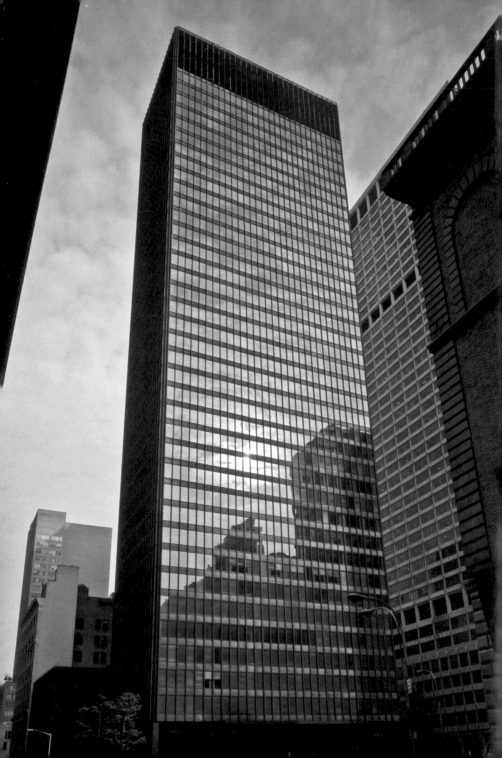

...isms

UNDERSTANDING
ARCHITECTURAL STYLES

JEREMY MELVIN

UNIVERSE

Contents

Architecture is all around us. Its connection to the immediate and everyday means it affects the patterns of our lives in both profound and subtle ways – for example, where we enter a building and how we move through it – evoking powerful memories, feelings, ideas and associations.

Yet architecture varies enormously according to time, place and social context. Such variations help us to place each type of architecture within one of the many different 'isms' used to describe particular periods of the subject's history.

This book is a simple guide to understanding the most important isms. The differences between them tend to be rooted in physical conditions, such as the purpose of a building, local climate and the availability of materials. Over time, these influences evolve into conventions, their features becoming intertwined with local culture, often generating long-lasting traditions. Through various routes, such as trade with other countries, these indigenous traditions may begin to influence societies and cultures elsewhere in the world, just as the Europeans took their architecture to their colonies.

If architecture's origins lay in humankind's need to create a habitat appropriate to prevailing conditions, it quickly became a way of negotiating and understanding such circumstances – of presenting a face to the gods and the natural elements they controlled. This characteristic continues today: architecture can help us to relate to our friends, neighbours and visitors, and to appreciate our place in society.

This book will help you to understand some of the major movements in architecture, and the concepts, physical and social conditions that underlie them. Though it does not provide a definitive checklist for identifying to which ism any given building might belong, it does suggest how architects may use a particular aesthetic to solve practical problems and, simultaneously, to express ideas.

There is no single definition of an ism. For example, some architects and buildings sit comfortably within more than one classification. Here, we have divided the isms into the five basic categories described opposite. Some remain relatively constant for long periods, in the case of Confucianism reflecting the consistency of the Chinese architectural tradition and static social order promoted by Confucius rather than China's actual political history. Others, like Indism, span similar time frames, but refer more to the way an architectural tradition can depend as much on change, adaptation and absorption as on stasis. Still more reflect the rapidity with which ideas can emerge, or at least be picked up by architects, only to be superseded by newer, more palatable isms within a decade or two. Finally, isms can co-exist, with even apparently contradictory ones like Monumental Urbanism and Medievalism addressing the same challenges of the 19th century.

Before the mid-19th century, architects did not think of themselves as practising a particular ism. They were not aware of such distinctions within architecture, despite the obvious differences between the various architects and the movements they represented. But from the 1830s onwards, architecture became increasingly politicised, and the choice of style ideological. By the early 20th century, subscribing to a particular movement had become de rigueur. However, more recently, architects have again begun to resist such categorisation.

THE FIVE TYPES OF ISM

1 BROAD CULTURAL TREND
e.g. Humanism, Neoclassicism

These isms are those where general cultural movements generated particular movements in architecture or, more occasionally, where an architectural movement set a new cultural standard. They would almost always have counterparts in other arts, and there may have been considerable cross-fertilisation between them. Though they may not have been long-lived, such isms are marked by a broad and simultaneous spread of similar ideas.

2 ARTIST-DEFINED MOVEMENT
e.g. Purism, Structuralism

Most of these isms date from the 19th and 20th centuries. These were periods when many architects found it increasingly important to define themselves and their ideas. Where possible, they joined forces with other architects to assert their values over any other contemporary movement, and generally over the past as well, often via published manifestoes. Though often characterised by eloquent rhetoric, they tended to lack the depth of intellectual tradition of less consciously defined isms.

3 RETROSPECTIVELY APPLIED LABEL
e.g. Proto-Classicism, Mannerism

This label is a boon to historians in organising what at the time may have seemed random and unrelated occurrences. For example, the builders of Knossos can hardly have thought of themselves as Proto-Classical. To do so they would have required a concept of Classicism that did not yet exist! But it is undeniable that their beliefs and practices helped to form Classicism, which in its various manifestations has been the most influential single architectural style. Thus, retrospectively applied labels are vital tools for understanding how trends coalesced, unwound and evolved over time.

4 REPRESENTATION OF AN IDEOLOGY
e.g. Pietism, Totalitarianism

All art has the potential to express an ideology more or less explicitly. However, the relationship between architecture and ideology is unique. Architecture, certainly when it becomes a building, lands someone with a bill. The larger the work of architecture, the richer and more powerful the individual behind it is likely to be and, consequently, the greater will be his or her concern to promulgate his or her own ideas.

5 REGIONAL OR NATIONAL TREND
e.g. Shintoism, Usonianism

Until technology made it possible to transport materials vast distances, and to artificially modify the climate within a building, architecture could scarcely escape a close connection to its surroundings. The interaction between the ideas and beliefs of a particular society, a given climate and topography, and immediately available building materials, often resulted in recognisable architectural traditions. These are best described as regional or national trends. During the 19th century, such historical traditions were frequently tied up with greater questions of national identity.

BCT Symbols are used to distinguish between the five different types of ism outlined in the introduction. This means you can tell at a glance whether an ism is a broad cultural trend BCT, an architect-defined movement ADM, a retrospectively applied label RAL, a representation of ideology RI, or a regional or national trend RNT.

INTRODUCTION
The first section of each ism is a brief introduction to the ism, giving a succinct summary of its main features.

KEY ARCHITECTS
This is a list of the most important architects related to the ism. Given the paucity of information for the Ancient & Pre-Renaissance isms, it is omitted in the first section.

KEY WORDS
These words sum up the key concepts, styles or issues relating to the ism. The key words provide a map of associations that will help you to quickly chart an ism and enable easier recollection of it.

MAIN DEFINITION
The main definition explores the ism in more depth than the brief introduction, explaining its significance, history and the ideas, methods or stylistic features that distinguish the ism from, or relate it to, other isms.

KEY BUILDINGS
Each ism is illustrated with one or two key buildings. These exemplify the principal features of the ism described in the rest of the text.

Inventionism **RAL**

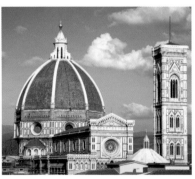

architecture. To complete his task he had to build from a Gothic base and devise ingenious construction techniques to achieve what became Europe's largest dome at its completion in 1436. Many of his solutions were controversial, but his success showed that new, empirically derived methods of building could produce results that had proved impossible when following precedent.

Brunelleschi essentially brought Classical discipline to given problems through ingenuity and experiment. His Ospedale degli Innocenti (1419–24) achieves a far more convincing Classical colonnade than the Loggia dei Lanzi, constructed in his youth, while San Lorenzo and Santo Spirito adapt Classicism to the traditional Gothic church plan. His friends Masaccio and Donatello redefined painting and sculpture in similar ways, while his follower Michelozzo di Bartolommeo (generally known as Michelozzo Michelozzi) created the precedent for the Renaissance palace in his Palazzo Medici (1444–59), introducing order and symmetry to this most important Renaissance building type.

The tradition of experiment and scientific inquiry continued throughout the Renaissance, alongside the revival of Classical learning, reaching its apogee in Leonardo da Vinci's explorations of issues such as flight and the human body, his notebooks containing some of the earliest investigations of what became a hallmark of the High Renaissance – the centrally planned church.

KEY BUILDINGS

Basilica di Santa Maria del Fiore (Florence Cathedral), Italy, FILIPPO BRUNELLESCHI, 1418–36
Brunelleschi's dome dominates not just the cathedral, but also the city's skyline and even the Arno Valley. No one had built a dome on this scale before, and Brunelleschi invented new construction techniques and equipment from his empirical knowledge of both Gothic and Roman architecture.

Palazzo Medici, Florence, Italy, MICHELOZZO DI BARTOLOMMEO, 1444–59
The Medici, an aristocratic family of merchants and bankers who ruled Florence in the 15th century, introduced a completely new concept of urban living with this palazzo. Previously, urban oligarchies lived in sprawling agglomerations of buildings whose size and height proclaimed their power and prestige. The palazzo type was in many ways less practical, yet it provided an opportunity to show wealth and authority through knowledge of Classical and Humanist learning, rather than dimensions alone.

Inquiry and experiment were as important in the early Renaissance as the new emphasis on Classical learning. This spirit of invention helped to transform perceptions of buildings from the techniques of their construction to the functional roles and symbolic meanings they could carry. Inventionism is a counterpart to the way perspective completely altered the scope of painting for pictorial representation.
FILIPPO BRUNELLESCHI (1377–1446); LORENZO GHIBERTI (1378–1455); MICHELOZZO DI BARTOLOMMEO (1396–1472); LEONARDO DA VINCI (1452–1519)

innovation; experimentation; challenge; novelty; construction craft.

By the early 15th century, Florence was wealthy enough to attempt what had previously been impossible. The greatest symbol of this, itself an emblem of the entire Florentine Renaissance, was Filippo Brunelleschi's cupola on the city's cathedral. Started as a Gothic structure in 1296, by 1418 construction had reached the point where the problem of spanning the 138-foot-wide crossing (the junction between the nave and transepts) could no longer be ignored. Brunelleschi was a goldsmith by trade, but had investigated Ancient Roman

OTHER BUILDINGS
ITALY: Loggia dei Lanzi, Florence, 1376–82; Baptistry doors, Florence, LORENZO GHIBERTI, 1401–24; Ospedale degli Innocenti, Florence, FILIPPO BRUNELLESCHI, 1419–24; Pazzi Chapel, Florence, FILIPPO BRUNELLESCHI, 1429–46; Santo Spirito, Florence, FILIPPO BRUNELLESCHI, 1445–82

Structural Rationalism; Neoclassicism; Humanism; Idealism; Gothic Scholasticism

Medievalism; Baroque; Rococo

OTHER BUILDINGS

This list is a supplement to the Key Buildings. The Other Buildings are also good examples of the ism, and where possible are geographically close to one or other of the key buildings, allowing you to explore an ism in one visit.

SEE ALSO

Isms are often inter-related. Those listed under See Also share an affinity, idea or method with the ism under discussion …

DON'T SEE

… And isms are often antithetical to each other! Or predicated on mutually exclusive, and incompatible, assumptions, methods or ideas. The isms listed under Don't See are, in some way, out of tune with the ism being discussed.

Other resources included in this book

GLOSSARY OF BUILDINGS

This is an alphabetical list of buildings, giving locations and dates, and the ism each one exemplifies most closely. Note that the list is not exhaustive, and does not cover all of the architectural riches in these countries.

GLOSSARY OF ARCHITECTS

Artists who have been identified as Key Architects are gathered in this alphabetical list for ease of reference. The Glossary of Architects also includes dates of birth and death, as well as the ism or isms with which the architect is most closely identified.

GLOSSARY OF USEFUL TERMS

The Glossary of Useful Terms contains technical terms that have been used in definitions of isms (i.e. crossing) as well as a general selection of terms that have not been used in the definitions (i.e. emergence technology), but which you may come across as you visit buildings or read about them in more detail elsewhere.

CHRONOLOGY OF ISMS

The chronology shows the lifespan of all of the isms covered in the book. Regional and national trends tend to be the longest lasting. One reason for this is that they are usually part of the way particular cultures adapt to the climate and geography of where they settle, and these responses become engrained in their cultural traditions. Even where they embrace change, they have a strong bearing on national identity and social structure. By the same token, broad cultural trends typically move at the pace of social change in general. Isms in both of these categories are likely to last longer than those defined by architects themselves (by a single architect or a group of architects) for a particular purpose. Isms that represent particular ideologies may be short-lived or long-lived, depending on the duration of the ideology. They can, on occasion, recur, though this does not necessarily imply a revival of the original style. Similarly, historians or critics may coin a new term to define a manageable subject for study, and to identify it vis-á-vis cotemporary movements, and those that immediately precede or succeed it.

PLACES TO VISIT

This gives approximate locations where examples of particular isms can be found. The list is by no means exhaustive. Rather, it is a selection of the types of architectural isms the visitor can expect to see in the major cities of the world.

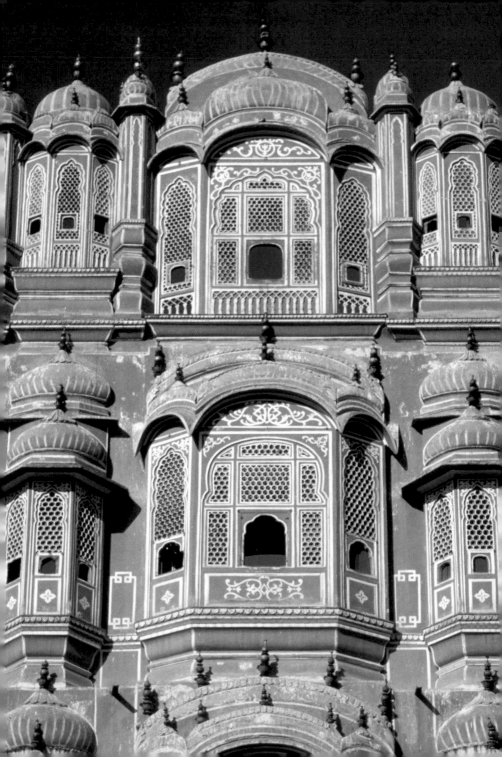

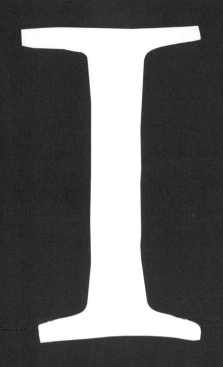

ANCIENT &
PRE-RENAISSANCE

Despite generic similarities such as a surplus food supply that often depended on favourable natural elements, early civilisations tended to emerge in isolation from each other and to develop different characteristics. However, the civilisations of the ancient Middle East were in such close proximity that they began to interact from an early date, and eventually contributed to, and accepted, influences from Hellenic Classicism.

monumentality; preservation; commemoration; slave labour; civilisation

Throughout the second and third millennia BC, climatic conditions and the availability of water from rivers across the ancient Middle East provided the necessary stability for numerous civilisations to develop. Of these, the most influential and long lasting was in Egypt, where regular floods from the River Nile made strips of the

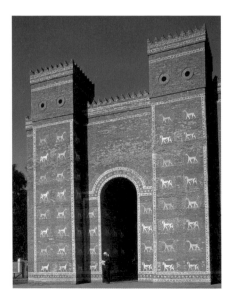

desert on either side fertile. Humans settled here from the earliest times, their artefacts gradually becoming more sophisticated until, at the start of the third millennium, they began to make structures whose ruins have survived to the present day. The most notable remains are tombs and temples, which reflects Ancient Egypt's theocratic foundation. The evolution of such creations also gives an insight into the changing balance of power between kings and priests.

The most familiar Egyptian monuments, the pyramids, developed from the first examples early in the third millennium, and culminated in the Great Pyramids of Giza, completed around 2500 BC. These royal tombs symbolised the passage of the Pharaoh from human to divine life. After 2000 BC came a stream of temples, such as that of Amon at Karnak. Built over many hundreds of years under successive kings, Amon is a monument to the evolution of particular beliefs rather than individual monarchs. In using features like columns with decoration derived from nature, yet with symbolic significance, it foreshadows Classicism. However, the predominance of funerary monuments in Ancient Egypt led to its popular association, in the 19th century, with death.

Traces of similar-aged civilisations are also found in Mesopotamia, where the two main rivers, the Tigris and the Euphrates, and their various tributaries nurtured numerous smaller states that never achieved the unity or continuity of Egypt. Many buildings were constructed with sun-baked bricks. However, their monumental architecture, marked by large volumes and massive walls, gradually acquired sophisticated surface decoration and, from the 4th century BC, as in Egypt, there was increasing interaction with the emerging Hellenic civilisation of Greece.

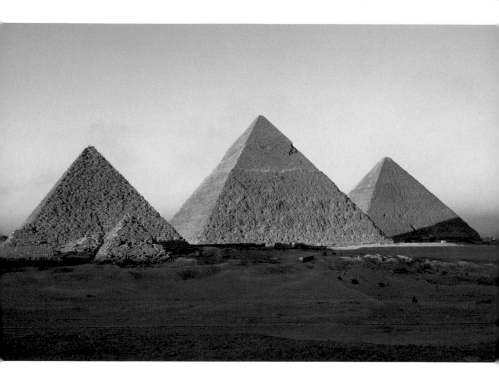

KEY BUILDINGS

 The Great Pyramids, Giza, outside Cairo, Egypt, c. 2631–2498 BC

From left: Mykerinos, Chephren and Cheops. Arguably the most famous, and certainly the largest of the monuments to have survived from antiquity, Cheops is almost 150 metres tall. The Giza pyramids were royal tombs, and their organisation reflects Egyptian beliefs about the transition to an afterlife. They are orientated to the cardinal compass points; each face is a near-equilateral triangle, and their layout reflects the pattern of key constellations.

← Ishtar Gate, Babylon, Mesopotamia, 605–563 BC

'Humankind will gaze with wonder', wrote Nebuchadnezzar II about the Ishtar Gate, part of his rebuilding of the city of Babylon. Glazed brickwork provides decorative patterning on this otherwise massive masonry, evoking Ishtar, the Egyptian goddess of war and unrestrained sexuality, and her sacred animal, the lion.

OTHER BUILDINGS

EGYPT Step Pyramid of Zoser, Saqqara, 2778–2723 BC; North and South Pyramids of Seneferu, Dahshur, 2723 BC; The Sphinx, Giza, c. 2600 BC; Great Temple of Amon, Karnak, 1530–323 BC; Temple of Luxor, 1408–1300 BC

MESOPOTAMIA Ziggurat and Precinct of Ur, rebuilt 2125 BC; Cities of Ashur, Nimrud and Khorsabad, 1250–700 BC

 Proto-Classicism; Pre-Columbianism; Indism; Confucianism; Sublimism

Gothic Scholasticism; Rococo; Neoclassicism; Rationalism

For several thousands of years, Indian architecture has evolved through the interaction between local and indigenous traditions and foreign influences. Its succession of cultures have shown a remarkable ability to absorb ideas from one tradition and transform them to suit the needs of another. This has resulted in an extraordinary diversity that nonetheless maps the subcontinent's rich cultural history.

cultural synthesis; masonry; Hinduism; Buddhism; Islam

As befits a large and densely populated subcontinent, architecture in India varies widely according to region and shows traces of numerous influences. The River Indus in modern Pakistan nurtured one of the world's oldest civilisations from the middle of the third millennium BC to a high point early in the second. It gave rise to several large urban settlements and left traces far beyond the valley of the river and its tributaries, though written records are scant and undecipherable. Subsequently, and with increasing intensity from about the 4th century BC, Indian architecture has shown a remarkable ability to incorporate foreign influences, evolving through

a process of mutual adaptation between new ideas and indigenous or established customs.

This is especially clear in religious buildings. Hinduism, the oldest of the great Indian religions, emerged as religious practice switched from sacrificial rituals to worship. Its early architecture derived from obscure mathematical formulae known only to the dominant priestly caste. Buddhism and Jainism arose partly as reactions to this theocracy, and their religious practices needed a new sort of architecture. Buddhism introduced congregational worship, requiring different spaces to the individual devotions of Hinduism, and also evolved the stupa (or tope), a shrine containing the ashes of those who fulfilled the Buddhist aim of achieving Enlightenment. Meeting these needs provided the incentive to accept foreign influences from Persia, and even Hellenic Classicism, which reached India via Alexander the Great in the 4th century BC.

The arrival of Islam from the 12th century AD onwards resulted in a flowering of this evolutionary characteristic of Indian architecture. While Islamic prescriptions regarding naturalistic representation had a profound effect on decoration, the propensity for integrating architectural tradition with religious practice continued. In his new capital, Fatehpur Sikri (1569–80), the Mughal Emperor Akbar sort to incorporate Islamic, Buddhist, Hindu and even Gothic decoration in symbolic unity. His grandson, Shah Jehan, built the Taj Mahal, the epitome of architecture that is both Indian and Islamic.

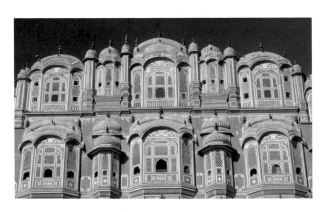

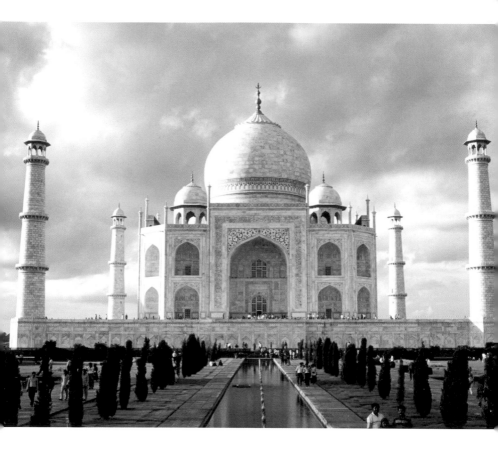

KEY BUILDINGS

↑ Taj Mahal, Agra, India, 1630–53

A shimmering vision of inlaid white marble, inset with coloured stones and surrounded by a formal garden, the Taj Mahal is a tribute to Shah Jehan's love for his favourite wife Mumtaz Mahal. As the greatest of the Mughal tombs, it is both the most familiar work of Indian architecture and the embodiment of its capability to fuse various traditions and influences.

← Hawa Mahal, Jaipur, Rajasthan, India, 1799

Part of the maharajah's city palace, this structure is also known as the Palace of the Winds. Though used here for a Hindu Rajput prince, the *jali* – or fretwork – was a Mughal innovation. Its main purpose was to allow and even accelerate air movement through the building without revealing views of the interior, making it an appropriate feature for the women's quarters.

OTHER BUILDINGS

INDIA Mohenjaro-daro and Harappa, Indus Valley, mid-third millennium BC; Qutb Minar, Delhi, 1199; Fatehpur Sikri, Agra, 1569–80; Humayun's Tomb, Delhi, 1585; Amber Palace, Rajasthan, 1623–68; Janta Manta, Jaipur, Rajasthan, 1726–34

 Indo-Khmerism; Confucianism; Islamicism; Regionalism

 Neoclassicism; Corporatism

Once thought a mysterious and self-contained civilisation with no connection to neighbouring cultures, there is now overwhelming evidence that the Minoan culture of Crete and its Mycenaean counterpart on the Greek mainland were forerunners of Hellenic Classicism. Though architecturally different, these buildings evolved simultaneously with the earliest stirrings of Classical mythology and language.

cyclopean masonry; tomb; defence; city-state

In the 1950s, Michael Ventris showed that the Linear B script found on numerous tablets in the Palace at Knossos on Crete was an early dialect of Ancient Greece. This opened the door to new interpretations of the various cultures of the Eastern Mediterranean that predated Hellenic Classicism, and indicated that it had evolved out of them. Notable among these are the sites of Aegean culture across the islands and mainland of Greece, such as Knossos and Mycenae, which flourished in the middle of the second millennium BC. Some aspects of their history and civilisation

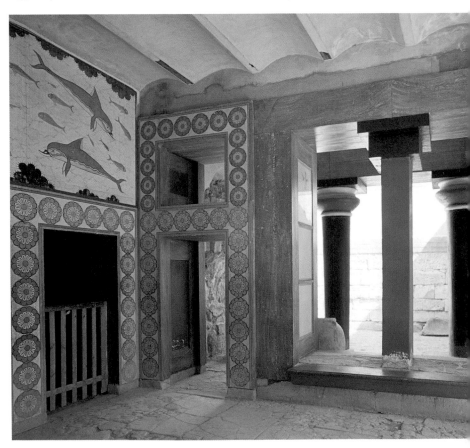

survive in Homer's *Illiad* and *Odyssey*.

The relationship between construction and decoration, as well as the purposes of those Proto-Classical buildings that have survived, differ from constructions of the Hellenic Classicism period in a number of ways. The principal remains are palace complexes, fortified citadels that evolved over long periods. Within them are distinct open and enclosed spaces, the emphasis seemingly on enclosures and interiors rather than on the exteriors of buildings, such as Classical temples, in public spaces.

Planning appears to follow practical needs rather than abstract geometrical patterns. Most construction is plain masonry, and painted interiors are the most common form of decoration. However, other than indicating how the spaces might have been used, this has little relationship to the architecture or construction, accept in rare instances, such as the Lion Gate at Mycenae. Here, a carved stone showing two lions is placed either side of a column resting on the lintel above the opening, creating a symbolic marker that may lend ritualistic or mythical significance to an important element of the building, such as the point of entry. Though much cruder, this heralds the balance between construction, decoration and function found in Classicism.

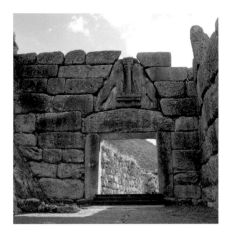

KEY BUILDINGS

←Palace of King Minos, Knossos, Crete, Greece, pre-1400 BC
The so-called Minoan civilisation of Crete was a forerunner of Hellenic Classicism, as was demonstrated by the discovery that the Linear B script of its inscribed tablets was an archaic form of Ancient Greek. Also influenced by Egypt, the palace marks an important point of cross-fertilisation between the civilisations of the ancient Eastern Mediterranean.

↑ Lion Gate, Mycenae, Greece, c. 1250 BC
Some 800 years before Hellenic Classicism reached its highpoint, the citadel at Tiryns gives some clues as to its early development. Though built out of massive and largely unadorned masonry, the giant lintel forming its main entrance gave an opportunity for a triangular decorative panel that would become an important feature in later Hellenic architecture.

OTHER BUILDINGS

GREECE Palace of Phaestos, Crete, 15th century BC; Treasury of Atreus, Mycenae, c.1300–1200 BC

 Pre-Classicism; Hellenic Classicism; Classicism; Sublimism

 Gothic Scholasticism; Rococo

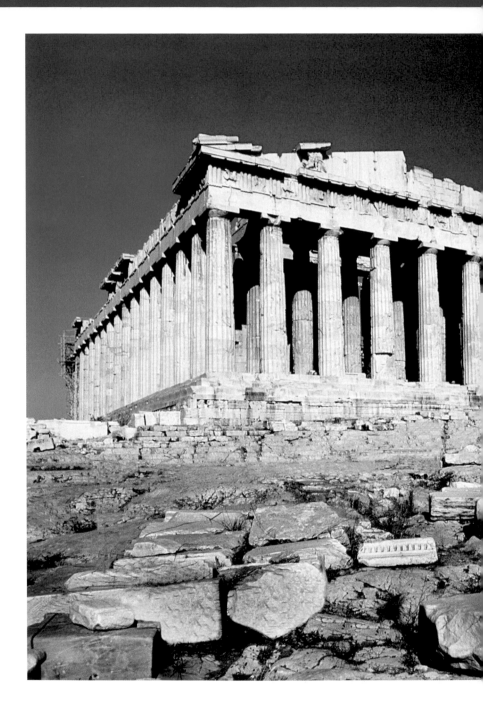

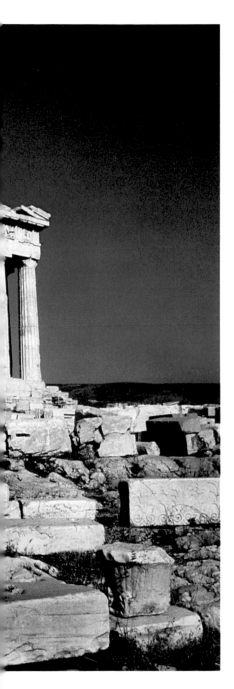

◔ Drawing on the achievements of Greek civilisation in general, Hellenic Classicism introduced new levels of sophistication to architectural expression. In particular it made mythical beliefs seem relevant to everyday experiences by combining familiar phenomena such as gravity with depictions of Classical mythology, an association that reinforced the idea that the society's belief system was rooted in reality.

◔ order; proportion; trabeation; entarsis; placement; polis; sacrifice; ritual

● Though there were larger buildings and greater feats of engineering than the Parthenon when it was built in the middle of the 5th century BC, none had the same symbolic, cultural and intellectual force. Hellenic Classicism has captivated almost every generation since, and inaugurated a tradition that lasted around 2,500 years. It shows how size and technical innovation, though important, are not enough to bestow the highest status on a work of architecture, and that to achieve such a status a building must also interact with intellect and emotion.

The Classical Orders of columns – Doric, Ionic and Corinthian – are the key to Greek architecture. Their origins are lost in mythology but they have precise rules for proportion and ornament, a combination

KEY BUILDINGS
◀—Parthenon, Athens, Greece, IKTINOS, 447–432 BC
The formula for a Classical temple of an exterior of columns with a pediment at either end may have its origins in primitive construction, but by the 5th century BC it had become incredibly sophisticated. Each element reflects its function, as well as having symbolic association, and is subtly shaped to correct optical illusions.

that means they are able to make tantalising allusions to cultural traditions and beliefs whilst also being subjected to intellectual discipline. Many features demonstrate this characteristic; for example, columns swell outwards slightly, as if being squashed as they rise from the base before tapering towards the capital, thus expressing as well as performing a load-carrying function. In mythology, Doric represents man, while Ionic depicts a matron and Corinthian a virgin. Thus the rules and traditions of the Orders transform the simple fact of gravity into a human condition.

Though the Orders are different, they share a balance between fact and allusion. For example, the Doric frieze in the Parthenon intersperses triglyphs with metopes: the former are stylised representations of the ends of timber beams and refer to the original wooden construction, and the latter are carved, often showing scenes from mythology.

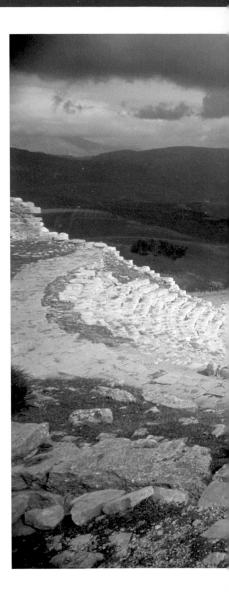

OTHER BUILDINGS

GREECE Olympia, from 590 BC; Corinth, from 540 BC; Delphi, from 510 BC; The Thesion (Hephaestion), Athens, 449–444 BC; Temple of Nike Apteros, Athens, 427 BC; The Erechtheion, Athens, 421–405 BC;

ITALY Various temples, Selinunte, Sicily, 550–450 BC; Temples of Paestum, near Naples, 530–460 BC; Various temples, Agrigento, Siciliy, 510–430 BC; Segesta Temple, Sicily, 424–416 BC

 Proto-Classicism; Roman Classicism; Neoclassicism; Shintoism

 Christian Classicism; Gothic Scholasticism; Indo-Khmerism

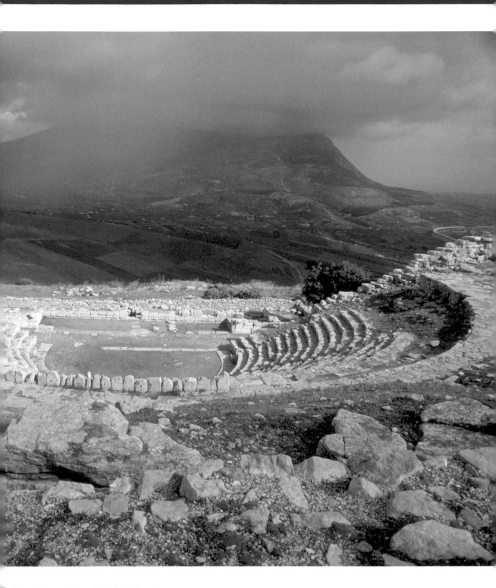

Segesta Theatre, Sicily, Italy, 3rd century BC
Drama helped the Ancient Greeks come to terms with
natural forces, thus the setting of their theatres was as
important as the plays performed in them. Curved tiers
of seating focused on a stage are typical and were well-
suited to the ritualised performances. At 63 metres in
diameter, this one is small, yet its symbolic connection
between human drama and nature is still obvious.

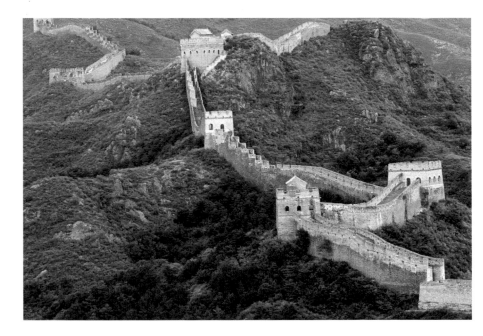

Architecture is one of the unifying characteristics of Chinese culture, varying little despite vast distances and huge differences in climate and landscape across the country, a stability that in part derives from the Confucian emphasis on social and moral order.

order; harmony; cosmos; authority; ancestor worship

Confucian philosophy values order and hierarchy above all other things, and its pervasive influence on Chinese culture over several millennia helped to maintain a remarkable homogeneity across a vast territory and its numerous peoples. Its effect on architecture is revealed in a strong continuity between buildings of very different ages, reflecting the static belief system, and in the way in which building form and urban planning convey Confucian cosmology. Each of the cardinal compass points has a mythical significance, which helps to place functions in relation to each other, and is the basis for feng shui.

Confucian cosmology and hierarchy merge in the belief that the emperor was the son of heaven and deserved unquestioning obedience. Thus, Confucianism confers great importance on temples and palaces, and most of all on structures that symbolise the imperial connection between heaven and earth. Individual buildings and entire cities share the same basic planning principles of regularity and order. Outside the cities, the landscape is dramatic and varied, but bridges over the numerous waterways, often of daring construction, are evidence of previous communication between different parts of the empire.

The roof is the most important element in Chinese architecture, often highly elaborated with distinctive upturned eaves.

The frame was constructed first, and this determined the position of the columns. Timber was the most common building material, supplemented with bricks, tiles and, in areas where it could easily be found, stone. In the 18th century, when European travellers started to visit China regularly, the combination of exotic-looking buildings against dramatic landscapes became an important source of inspiration for new aesthetic ideas.

Social and political stability allowed China to absorb influences from outside, of which Buddhism was the most important, but from early times trade, especially in silk, brought contact with Europe. Whatever could not be absorbed was considered barbarian, and keeping barbarians at bay gave rise to the largest single feat of Chinese construction, the 2,260-kilometre-long Great Wall, built in successive phases from 214 BC to protect China's northern frontier.

KEY BUILDINGS

← **The Great Wall of China, 214** BC
Stretching 2,260 kilometres and following the natural topography of the northern edge of the ancient Chinese Empire, the Great Wall is not only a vast undertaking, but also a powerful demonstration of the division between civilisation and barbarism, and the need to keep strict order within the boundaries of the Empire, whatever was happening beyond.

↓ **The Temple of Heaven, Beijing, China, 1420**
This complex of buildings was where the emperor would go to propitiate heaven, creating a symbolic connection that reinforced the Confucian social hierarchy. The circular prayer hall (on the right) typifies traditional Chinese timber construction and symbolism, the 28 columns representing 28 constellations, as well as months and periods of the day.

OTHER BUILDINGS
CHINA South Pagoda, Fang-Shan, Hopei, AD 117; Wild Goose Pagoda, Ch'ang-Ang, Shensi, AD 701–05; Imperial Palace, Forbidden City, Beijng, 1407–20

Indism; Indo-Khmerism; Shintoism; Exoticism

Hellenic Classicism; Gothic Scholasticism

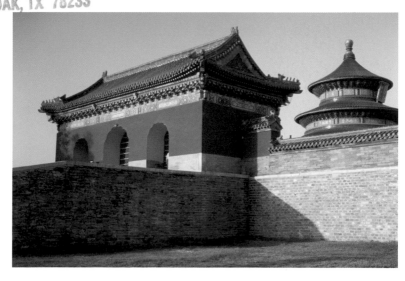

Roman Classicism

Though sharing many common beliefs with the Greeks, the Romans were faced with the task of administering and servicing a vast empire. Their society inevitably became more complex and required a wider range of building types in a greater variety of locations that could perform more tasks.

empire; power; arch; dome; interior

Beyond using the same Classical Orders of Doric, Ionic and Corinthian, Roman architecture is very different to Greek. Where Greek cities were often sited with symbolic potential in mind, Roman cities generally derive from the gridded plan of a military camp. In construction and decoration, the two forms of architecture are even further apart. Roman architecture introduced the arch and, eventually, the dome, which made possible more types, and greater sizes of space. This opened the door to buildings with complex combinations of spaces, such as the Baths of Caracalla and Hadrian's Villa.

Roman architecture also combines the Orders with a freedom that would have shocked the Greeks, as it challenged their static worldview. For example, the plan of the Colosseum, a vast structure that the Greeks could never have envisaged, is an oval, its four tiers each having a different Order rising from Doric through Ionic to Corinthian, with the later addition of a Composite Order. The lower three tiers combine half columns with arches.

As a more complex, widespread and longer-lasting entity than the Greek city-states, the Roman Empire needed more building types and also had to overcome significant engineering challenges such as building roads and transporting water.

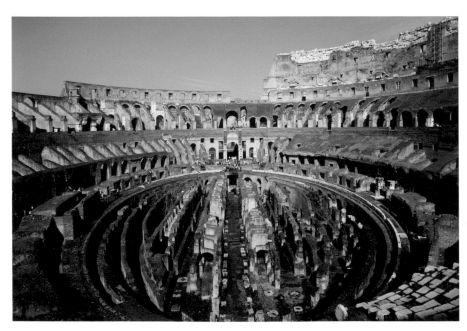

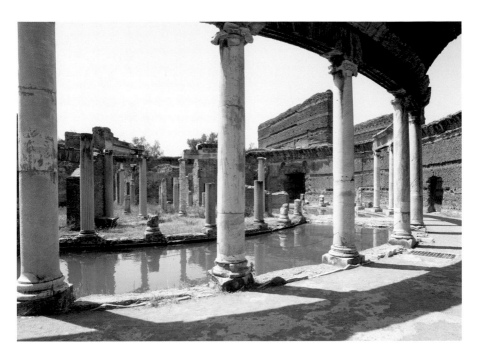

In addition, buildings to mark different events and rituals, like the Triumphal Arch to celebrate Imperial victories, needed to be created.

In summary, Roman architecture lost the taut relationship between nature, society and myth that Hellenic Classicism captured so strongly, but in its freer forms and compositions revealed how Classicism could adapt to different societies and purposes.

KEY BUILDINGS

← Colosseum, Rome, Italy, AD 70–82

A vast oval almost 200 metres long, and surrounded by a wall of 80 giant bays, the Colosseum could hold 50,000 spectators in addition to the wild beasts, gladiators and victims. Its sophisticated construction, adaptation of the Classical Orders and integration of them with an arcade, shows the monumentality that Roman architecture achieved, in part to reinforce the Imperial regime.

↑ Hadrian's Villa, Tivoli, Italy, AD 124

Roman architecture reflected the heterogeneity of its empire, and this Imperial villa consciously sought to represent its different traditions, becoming almost an index of the known world. Its various parts are juxtaposed according to the topography of the site rather than having an axial arrangement, and the Island Villa (pictured) is surrounded by variously shaped rooms, all unified by the central circular colonnade.

OTHER BUILDINGS

ITALY Theatre of Marcellus, Rome, 21–13 BC; Pompeii, destroyed AD 79; Arch of Titus, Rome, AD 82; The Pantheon, Rome, AD 118–26; Temple of Vesta, Rome, AD 205; Baths of Caracalla, Rome, AD 211–17; The Forum, Rome, 1st century BC–4th century AD

 Hellenic Classicism; Christian Classicism; Sublimism

 Shintoism; Gothic Scholasticism

Pre-Columbian America had several distinct cultures that European conquest ended but did not erase. Over the last century, through awakening interest in their cultural values as much as archaeological discoveries, these cultures have had some influence on contemporary architectural ideas.

monumentality; ritual; sacrifice; cosmology

At least two significant architectural traditions developed in America before Europeans reached the continent shortly before AD 1500. In Central America, Mayan civilisation evolved from the earlier Olmec culture, and left its mark in the form of numerous stepped-pyramid temples, often set in precincts that emphasise their monumental character. The Aztecs developed Mayan architectural forms, and adapted them to new and blood-curdling religious rituals. Stonework, used on all important buildings, was sophisticated but limited in range: for example, arches were unknown at the time. Instead, corbelling developed to a high degree, along with stylised and geometrical carving.

Further south, in the area roughly covered by modern Peru, Inca civilisation flourished in the millennium before the Spanish conquest of 1532. It developed into a highly centralised empire with a rigid and hierarchical social order. Its main architectural monuments reflect its predication on the belief that the Inca (emperor) was related to the Sun god. Orientation to catch the sun at particular times to mark important rituals is an important feature of Inca architecture, which is generally plainly decorated but marked by masonry of exquisite quality. In the narrow strip of land between the Pacific Ocean and the Andes, adobe brick is the most common material, while in the mountains stone is more plentiful. Engineering was an important part of Inca construction, and included roads to assist the administration of a vast empire, and terraces cut into mountainsides to carve out as much cultivatable land as possible.

The Pueblo Indians developed a far simpler architectural tradition in what is now the southwest of the US. Though they often used mud bricks, which wash away over time, the vast housing complex of Pueblo Bonito in New Mexico (c. 900–1200) uses finely dressed local stone.

KEY BUILDINGS

→ Machu Picchu, near Cuzco, Peru, c.1500
Shortly before the Spanish conquest of their empire in 1532, the Incas built this spectacularly sited mountain city. Their skill in masonry is obvious in the buildings and the terracing of the mountainside to make land for cultivation, while orientation of the buildings to the sun reflects its role in their interlinked religious and social order.

OTHER BUILDINGS

MEXICO Pyramid of the Sun, Teotihuacán, c. AD 250; Citadel, Teotihuacán, c. AD 600; Temple of the Warriors, Chichen Itza, c.1100; Ball Court, Chichen Itza, c. 1200

PERU Gate of the Sun, Tiahuanaco, c.1000–1200; Cuzco, 1450–1532; Sacsayhuamán, c.1475

Pre-Classicism: Proto-Classicism; Indo-Khmerism

Gothic Scholasticism; Neoclassicism

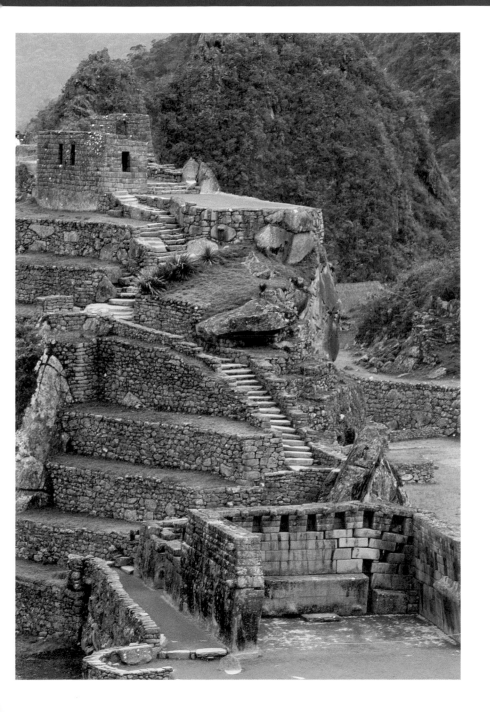

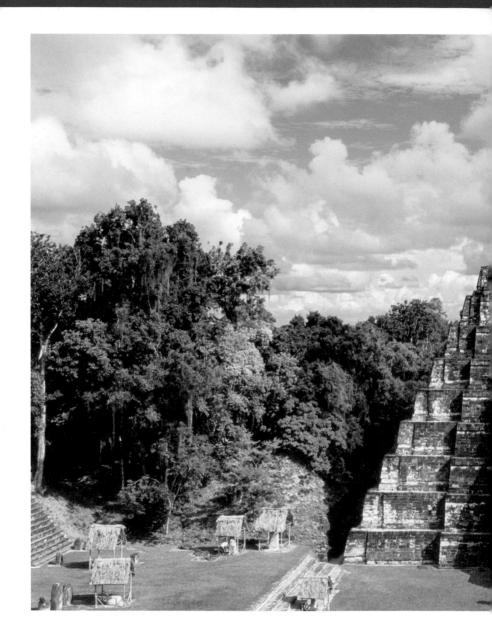

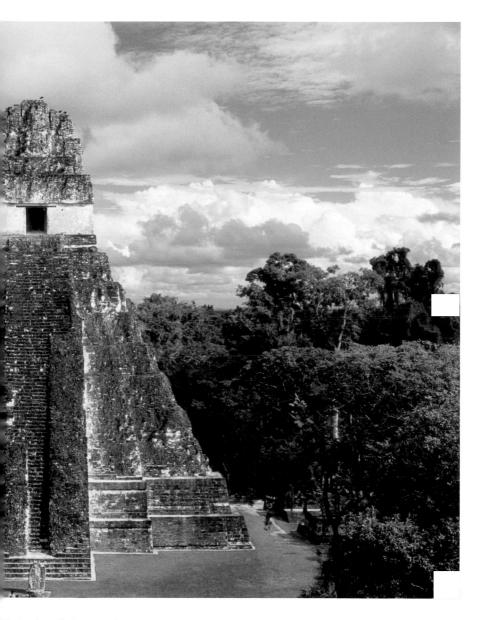

↑ **Temple 1, Tikal, Guatemala, c. AD 500**
The Mayans used stepped pyramids as the bases for temples. This one shows many of their typical features. The temple is reached by a single flight of steps that rises 30 metres through 10 separate tiers, the elaborate temple structure above the massive masonry pyramid emphasising the monumental character.

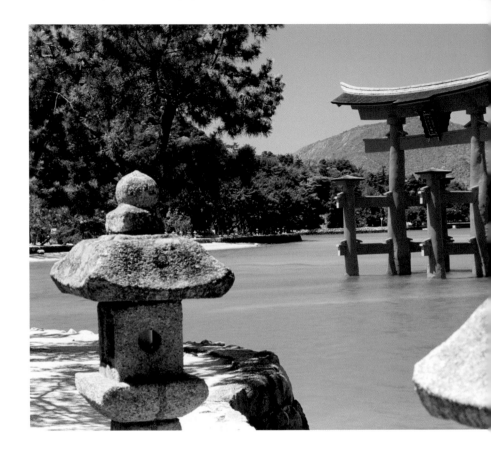

Shinto is an ancient Japanese belief system that promotes ancestor and nature worship. It has remained an important influence on Japanese culture, providing a common, indigenous theme for absorbing foreign influences.

lightness; delicacy; craftsmanship; nature

Japan takes the balance between nature and culture that underlies most architecture to the extreme. The natural topography creates dramatic landscapes of mountains, lakes, cliffs and the ocean, while the cultural tendency towards isolationism – all foreign influences were excluded between the early 17th- and mid-19th centuries – meant that architectural ideas, once introduced, developed independently of other national traditions.

The ancient belief system of Shinto formed Japanese practices of nature and ancestor worship without creating a particular architectural identity. The arrival of Buddhism from China during the 6th century brought both an impetus to build and a way of building that account for the similarities between Japanese and Chinese architecture. But just as Buddhism never

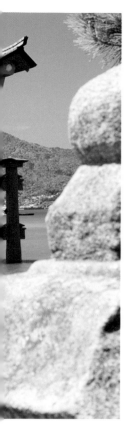

completely eclipsed Shintoism, so Japanese architecture, though it had taken on board the Chinese pattern of timber structure and the overwhelming importance of the roof, began to develop its own character. Decorative art in many Japanese media reached a high level of refinement, while architectural composition started to exploit the effects of symmetry and asymmetry, and the possibilities of creating a subtle balance between them. Building types began to evolve for specifically Japanese rituals, such as the tea ceremony.

These attributes gradually gave Japanese architecture an extremely sophisticated sense of composition. Every element has its correct place and size, but is dependent on the complex interrelation of each component rather than on an abstract sense of symmetry or geometry. In this way, nature and social hierarchy seem to merge, implying that the latter is a product of the former.

KEY BUILDINGS

←Floating Torii Gate, Itsukushima Jinja Shrine, Miyajima, Japan, 12th century
Shintoism is a religion of polytheistic nature worship, and its architecture strives for a balance between artifice and nature. This gateway symbolically links distant mountain-tops with the sea, framing the view as if bringing them closer together. The shrine, comprising several structures, was founded by Taira no Kiyomori, at the time the most powerful figure in Japan.

↓ Imperial Villa, Katsura, Japan, KOBORI ENSHU, 1620
Prince Toshihito, a younger brother of the emperor at the time (Emperor Goyozei), took the 10th-century novel *The Tale of the Genji* as the inspiration for his villa complex. Its architecture aims for simplicity and a close relationship with nature, in both its immediate setting and in the views that its landscape planning contrives. In the 20th century, European Modernists saw it as the essence of Japanese tradition.

OTHER BUILDINGS

JAPAN Shinto shrine of Kamiji-Yama, Ise, AD 701; Imperial Palace, Nara, 8th century AD; Kasuga Shrine, Nara, AD 768 onwards

 Confucianism; Metabolism; Indo-Khmerism

 Pre-Classicism; Hellenic Classicism; Sublimism

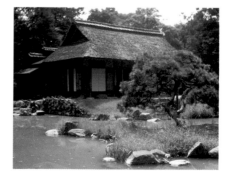

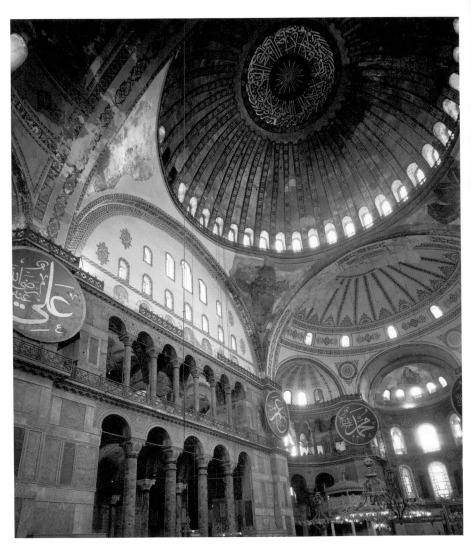

Christianity was already almost 300 years old when the Romans adopted it as their official religion, and this was an event that would have a significant impact on the Empire's architecture and town planning. During centuries of repression, Christian beliefs and practices had hardened, but the meeting places for such worship had to remain a secret to prevent discovery, and their architecture was deliberately modest. Classical architecture was certainly monumental, but it had evolved from, and reinforced, pagan beliefs. The challenge was to develop an architecture that was both monumental and Christian.

⏺ Christianity; Catholicism; orthodoxy; doctrine; martyrology; simplicity; figurative decoration

● As precedents for churches, temples were clearly inappropriate, but the great domed structures of Imperial Rome did have some relevance. They could create large interiors for many worshippers; their circular geometry could be understood as referring to the unity and perfection of God; and their form could create a sense of mystery through lighting effects such as the oculus at the apex of the Pantheon's dome (AD 118–126), as well as having some affinities with the sort of sepulchral spaces with which Christians were familiar. From the early 6th century, great domed churches such as Hagia Sophia in Constantinople (the new 'Christian' Rome) and San Vitale in Ravenna used Classical details in essentially new forms, their extensive wall spaces giving scope for devotional mosaic decoration.

A further development took place when the orthodox and Catholic traditions of Christianity split irrevocably. Centralised, domed spaces suited the liturgical and mystical practices of orthodoxy, culminating in designs including Moscow's multiple-minareted St Basil's Cathedral (1554). With its more prescriptive liturgy, the Catholic tradition stressed the clergy's role as mediator between heaven and earth, or God and the people. The longitudinal plan, with a nave between the main, western entrance and the high altar at the eastern end, suited it better. By 1100, across Western Europe there were numerous examples of Romanesque churches with this plan form, their 'Roman' traces being round arches and vestigial Classical detail.

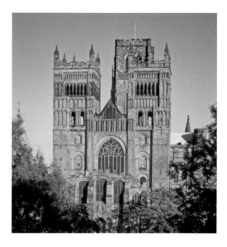

KEY BUILDINGS

↑ **Durham Cathedral, England, 1093–1132**
Durham represents the peak of Christian Classicism, or Romanesque, architecture, and by this date its connection with Ancient Classicism was quite vestigial, in the solid volumes of the exterior and rounded arches of the interior.

← **Hagia Sophia, Istanbul, Turkey, AD 532–7**
This massive and ingeniously constructed church was the highpoint of the Byzantine form of Christian Classicism. Interiors were more important in churches than in temples, and thus it adapts the arch and dome of Roman Classicism to Christian symbolism, such as light and ascent to heaven.

OTHER BUILDINGS
ITALY San Stefano Rotondo, Rome, AD 468–83; St Mark's Basilica, Venice, 1063–85

UK Chapel of St John, Tower of London, 1086–97; St Albans Abbey, 1077–1115

TURKEY St Sergius and St Bachus, Istanbul, AD 525–30; St Saviour in the Chora, Istanbul, 1050

 Roman Classicism; Gothic Scholasticism

 Hellenic Classicism; Neoclassicism

Islamic architecture hinges around the mosque, which, unlike a church, is not a representation of the divine but a tool to facilitate the duties of Muslims. As such it is much more than a place of worship; it is also a meeting point and a site for exchanging ideas, weaving religious practices into everyday experience.

geometry; axis; symmetry; pointed arch; vault; decoration

Islam mushroomed rapidly from its epicentre in the Arabian peninsular, in the early 7th century, across the Middle East, North Africa and into Western Europe via the Iberian peninsular. Its greatest architectural monuments can be found as far apart as Spain and India. The direct clarity of its message gave it broad appeal, and it quickly came into contact with many other cultures.

Mosques combine various activities that in the West are typically divided between separate buildings. Though their general organisation seeks to balance their various parts according to an abstract concept of perfect creation, they tend to reflect the clarity of Islamic doctrine with few prescriptions for their design beyond a requirement that worshippers face Mecca when praying, and a niche from where an imam leads prayers. However, the prohibition of representations of nature on religious grounds means that decoration tends to be stylised, offering opportunities for inventive geometrical patterns. Thus the architectural character of the Islamic mosque comes from the repetition of simple but sometimes richly decorated elements such

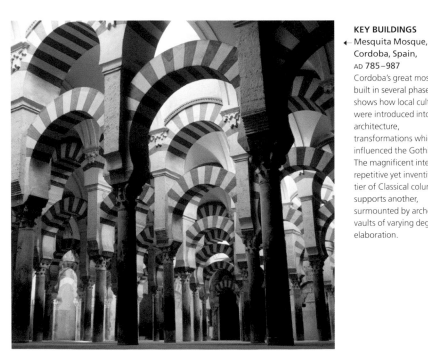

KEY BUILDINGS
← Mesquita Mosque, Cordoba, Spain, AD 785–987
Cordoba's great mosque, built in several phases, shows how local cultures were introduced into Islamic architecture, transformations which later influenced the Gothic era. The magnificent interior is repetitive yet inventive. One tier of Classical columns supports another, surmounted by arches and vaults of varying degrees of elaboration.

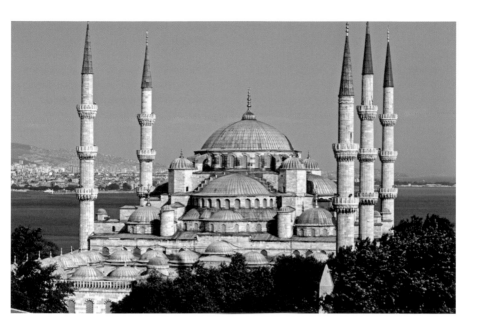

as columns, alongside features like minarets and domes from other cultures.

The size of mosques varies enormously, with the larger examples often including schools and accommodation for travellers, adding to their role as places for exchange of ideas and commerce. The tradition of scholarship this fostered meant that the Islamic world had much to teach medieval Europe, from copies of Ancient Classical texts to new ideas in fields like medicine and mathematics.

↑ Blue Mosque, Istanbul, Turkey, SEDEFKAR MEHMET AGHA, 1610–16

As the Ottoman Empire gradually replaced the Byzantine Empire, its architects incorporated domes – a hallmark of Byzantine orthodox churches – into their mosques. Agha's inspiration here was the greatest of all Byzantine buildings, the nearby Hagia Sophia, combining a series of domes with six minarets to create a sense of uplift.

OTHER BUILDINGS

MIDDLE EAST Dome of the Rock, Jerusalem, Israel, AD 684; Al-Aqsa Mosque, Jerusalem, Israel, AD 705; Great Mosque, Damascus, Syria, AD 706–15; Mosque of Al-Azhar, Cairo, Egypt, AD 970

SPAIN City of Madinat-al-Zahra (near Cordoba), AD 936; Alhambra Palace, Granada, 1338–90

 Gothic Scholasticism; Indism

 Hellenic Classicism; Neoclassicism

The great Indian religions of Hinduism and Buddhism inspired important architectural traditions that spread outwards across southeast Asia. Their diverse pantheons and rich religious texts were commemorated in lavishly carved buildings, whose positioning and massing is also related to their cosmology.

decoration; order; cultural exchange; cosmology

Emanating outwards from India from the third century BC, Hinduism and Buddhism took their architecture across southeast Asia. Often interacting with indigenous local cultures, they formed several distinct but related architectural traditions. One of the most important of these is the Khmer civilisation centred in

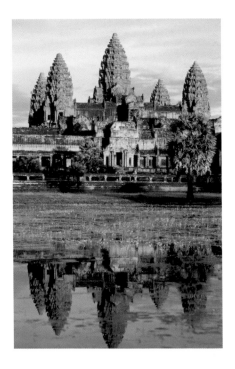

what is now Cambodia. Almost lost under the jungle, as it has been uncovered over the last 100 years its extraordinary forms and settings have contributed to visual culture.

In the 9th century AD, various Khmer states were unified under a single king. Over the subsequent 600 years, numerous settlements were constructed in the 300-square-kilometre area of Angkor, culminating in the 12th-century temple of Angkor Wat. This is the one part of the site that was not later swamped by jungle between the 16th and 20th centuries.

Architecture became the most important art in Khmer culture because it was the only medium that could add layers of symbolic meaning to the obvious function of such enormous structures. Control of the water supply helped to centralise power, and among Angkor's monuments are several giant reservoirs. Each reservoir had its own temple, often an island surrounded by water, which gave their practical purpose religious significance.

Khmer architecture was cosmological. Each building was a symbolic microcosm of the universe, an effect achieved through highly developed composition and decoration that evoke Khmer creation myths. Angkor Wat's central sanctuary rises from a platform surrounded by concentric plinths, as the cosmic mountain Meru arises from the heart of the central continent, which in turn was ringed by six continents and seven oceans. A stone wall encloses all. Each part, whether a large volume or a small decorative feature, has an ascribed place and function, and the effect of the decoration is to reinforce and elaborate, through naturalistic representation, the mythological message and status of each.

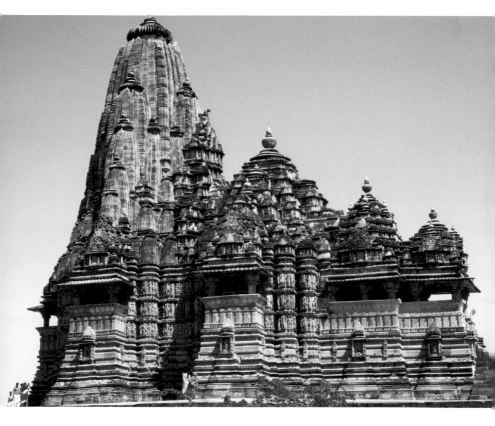

KEY BUILDINGS

Angkor Wat, Cambodia, early 12th century
Dedicated to the Hindu god Vishnu, the new temple at
Angkor was built by Suryavarman II. Dominated by its
central sanctuary, which is in turn surrounded by four
lower ones and an outer enclosure with four further
corner towers and a moat, its plan depicts concentric
cosmology, while the numerous surfaces and niches
provide ample opportunity for sculptural depictions of
sacred texts.

**Kandaraya Mahadev Temple, Khajuraho, India,
1017–29**
The Chandella Dynasty built a series of temples in its
capital, of which this is the largest and the most
elaborate. It also shows a relationship between religious
ritual and architectural symbolism that influenced temple
building across southeast Asia, with almost a thousand
statues illuminating tantric texts, and a Shiva-linga in the
interior.

OTHER BUILDINGS

INDIA Khajuraho, various temples, late 9th
century–11th century; Tanjavur and Rajarajeshvara
temples, 9th–13th centuries

CAMBODIA Various sites within the park at Angkor,
AD 802–1431; Preah Ko Temple, Angkor Wat, C. AD 880;
Preah Khan Temple, Angkor Wat, late 12th century

Indism; Confucianism; Gothic Scholasticism;
Pre-Columbianism

Hellenic Classicism; Neoclassicism

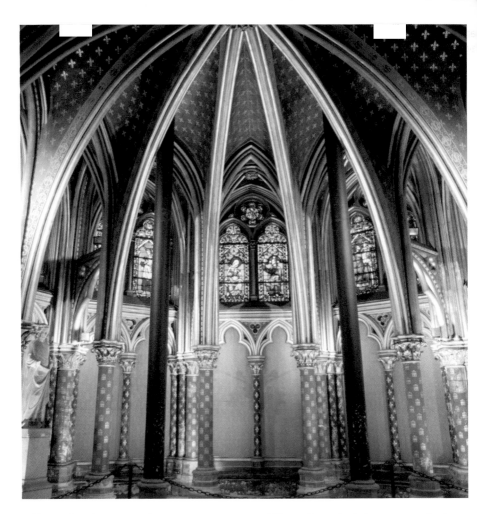

◐ Far from being a total opposite to Classical architecture, Gothic architecture draws heavily on Classical thinkers like Plato and Aristotle, and its proportions have some affinity with buildings of the Classical period. Where it differs is in its relationship to Christian theology.

◔ bible of the illiterate; light; transcendence; pointed arch; vault; stained glass

● Gothic cathedrals were conceived as depictions of heaven, and although earlier Christian architecture had attempted the same, the greater technical prowess and new thinking of the Middle Ages took Gothic architecture to a different dimension. The pointed arch and rib vaulting, developments of Islamic construction, fundamentally changed the relationship between structure, appearance and function. A wall could become a web of thin stone lines with light in between, rather than a solid surface. Every part of the structure seems to have a specific function. Walls no longer invited painted or inlaid decoration; instead, the carved shape of the stone elements is what gave expression.

These technical innovations were in keeping with medieval religious beliefs. Heaven had a perfection that earth could never match, but the purity of mathematics and the presence of light could convey something of divine beauty. With light streaming into cathedrals through increasingly elaborate stained-glass windows, and with the size and relationship between the different stone ribs governed by mathematical proportions, the architecture of this period had the potential to give a glimpse of heaven on earth.

Gothic architecture had a profound relationship with Scholastic thought, which represented the predominant approach to theology and philosophy in the Middle Ages, and the founding principles of many European universities. One of its aims was to explain the link between the perfection of heaven and the flawed earth, and increasingly sophisticated interpretive devices were developed as a result. Architecture, rooted in practical reality yet also seemingly in touch with the divine, provided an essential vehicle for connecting religious experience with everyday life through its layers of meaning.

KEY BUILDINGS
Sainte Chapelle, Paris, France, PIERRE DE MONTREUIL, 1243–8
Typifying the Gothic skeletal stone structure, the infill spaces of Sainte Chapelle are not masonry, but stained-glass windows that tell a story for those who want to look for it. The windows also bathe the interior with a transcendent luminosity which, whatever else it does, creates a very different ambience to outdoor space.

Rheims Cathedral, France, BERNARD DE SOISSONS, 1211–90
As the coronation church of the French kings, Rheims Cathedral is important even among the great Gothic cathedrals of northern France. Its west front has 500 sculptural figures organised to link biblical stories to French saints. Unlike their English counterparts, French cathedrals were not attached to monasteries, but instead closely integrated into their social and physical fabric.

OTHER BUILDINGS
FRANCE Abbey of St Denis, outside Paris, 1135–44; Notre Dame Cathedral, Paris, 1163–1250; Chartres Cathedral, 1194–1260

UK Canterbury Cathedral, 1096–1185; Lincoln Cathedral, 1129–1320; Westminster Abbey, London, 1245–late 14th century; Kings College Chapel, Cambridge University, 1446–1515

 Christian Classicism; Medievalism; Islamicism

 Hellenic Classicism; Neoclassicism; Rationalism

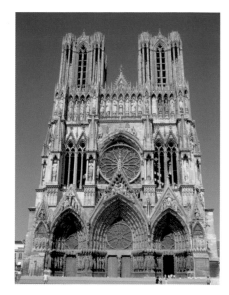

International trade helped the spread of ideas across Europe. Though it did not result in a single architectural style, the wealth it created helped to stimulate the emergence of secular architecture which, at its grandest, rivalled the great cathedrals for spectacle.

commerce; internationalism; decoration; invention

During the later Middle Ages, international trade grew to such an extent that it provided a network of contacts and exchange across Europe that was second only to the Roman Catholic Church as a unifying cultural force between its disparate states and varied frontiers. Where the Church needed cathedrals, monasteries and universities to proclaim its message, trading activity gave rise to guild- and town halls, market places and, by the end of the period, lavish homes for merchants to display their wealth.

Initially, civic and commercial architecture in the Middle Ages was more closely related to the vernacular of each region than the international Gothic of the great cathedrals. Prosperous wool towns like Lavenham in Suffolk, England, have numerous timber-

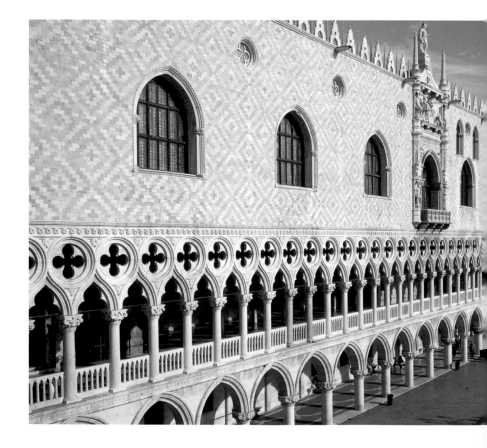

framed houses that are distinguished from neighbouring farmhouses by their elaborate decoration rather than any conceptual difference. But centres of international trade such as Flanders, Venice and the Hanseatic cities of northern Europe developed architectural styles that surpassed the vernacular completely. The gigantic cloth hall at Ypres in Belgium gives an indication of the extent of the wool trade that traversed northern Italy to England, while the great gateway to Lübeck, in Germany, is evidence not just of wealth, but also of the independence of mercantile cities from royal authority.

This reached its apogee in Venice, which created its own unique social order, and whose culture was closer to its Byzantine trading partners than its neighbours in Western Europe. The Venetian mercantile oligarchy developed an elaborately ornamental style for their own palaces, and especially the residence of their ruler, the Doge.

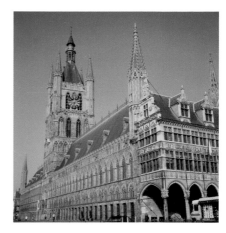

↑ Cloth Hall, Ypres, Belgium, 1202–1304
Rebuilt after the First World War, at 134 metres long the size of this cloth hall testifies to the wealth that spread to Ypres and other cities in Flanders via the international wool trade in the later Middle Ages. Though there are elaborate details, here the main effect comes from simplicity and repetition, showing how versatile Gothic architecture could be both in its range of expression and adaptability to different functions.

KEY BUILDINGS
 Doges Palace, Venice, Italy, GIOVANNI and BARTOLOMEO BUON, 1309–1424
Venice was one of the richest and most cosmopolitan mercantile cities in the Middle Ages, and its unique social structure and location on water brought about the adaptation of Gothic architecture into an exquisite yet carefully ordered expression of moral and material wealth. Here, the two-storeyed arcade of Doges Palace gave plenty of opportunity for inventive carving.

OTHER BUILDINGS
BELGIUM Cloth Hall, Bruges, 1282; Town Hall, Bruges, from 1376; Town Hall, Ghent, 1515–28

UK Guildhall, Lavenham, Suffolk, 1530; Market Cross, Salisbury, 14th century

 Medievalism; Victorianism; Gothic Scholasticism

 Neoclassicism; Sublimism

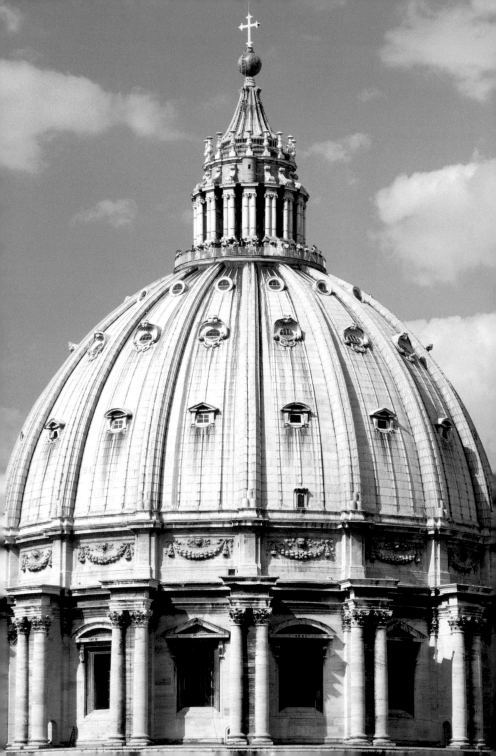

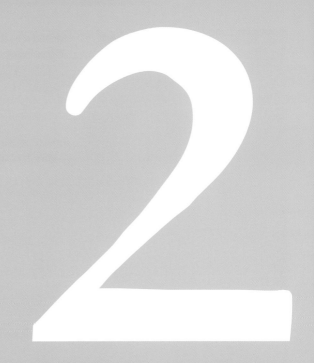

2

RENAISSANCE

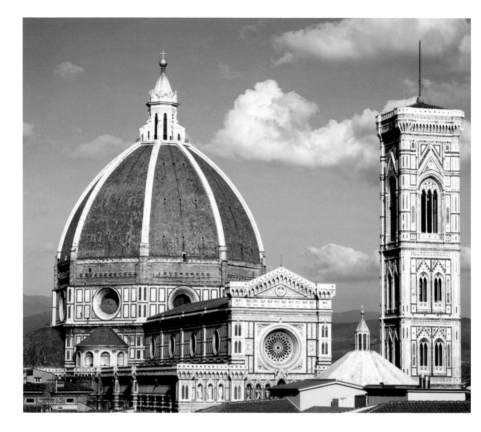

Inquiry and experiment were as important in the early Renaissance as the new emphasis on Classical learning. This spirit of invention helped to transform perceptions of buildings from the techniques of their construction to the functional roles and symbolic meanings they could carry. Inventionism is a counterpart to the way perspective completely altered the scope of painting for pictorial representation.

FILIPPO BRUNELLESCHI (1377–1446); **LORENZO GHIBERTI** (1378–1455); **MICHELOZZO DI BARTOLOMMEO** (1396–1472); **LEONARDO DA VINCI** (1452–1519)

innovation; experimentation; challenge; novelty; construction craft

By the early 15th century, Florence was wealthy enough to attempt what had previously been impossible. The greatest symbol of this, itself an emblem of the entire Florentine Renaissance, was Filippo Brunelleschi's cupola on the city's cathedral. Started as a Gothic structure in 1296, by 1418 construction had reached the point where the problem of spanning the 138-foot-wide crossing (the junction between the nave and transepts) could no longer be ignored. Brunelleschi was a goldsmith by trade, but had investigated Ancient Roman architecture. To complete his task he had to build from a Gothic base and devise ingenious construction techniques to achieve what became Europe's largest dome at its completion in 1436. Many of his solutions were controversial, but his success showed that new, empirically derived methods of building could produce results that had proved impossible when following precedent.

Brunelleschi essentially brought Classical discipline to given problems through ingenuity and experiment. His Ospedale degli Innocenti (1419–24) achieves a far more convincing Classical colonnade than the Loggia dei Lanzi, constructed in his youth, while San Lorenzo and Santo Spirito adapt Classicism to the traditional Gothic church plan. His friends Masaccio and Donatello redefined painting and sculpture in similar ways, while his follower Michelozzo di Bartolommeo (generally known as Michelozzi Michelozzo) created the precedent for the Renaissance palace in his Palazzo Medici (1444–59), introducing order and symmetry to this most important Renaissance building type.

The tradition of experiment and scientific inquiry continued throughout the Renaissance, alongside the revival of Classical learning, reaching its apogee in Leonardo da Vinci's explorations of issues such as flight and the human body, his notebooks containing some of the earliest investigations of what became a hallmark of the High Renaissance – the centrally planned church.

KEY BUILDINGS

← Basilica di Santa Maria del Fiore (Florence Cathedral), Italy, FILIPPO BRUNELLESCHI, 1418–36
Brunelleschi's dome dominates not just the cathedral, but also the city's skyline and even the Arno Valley. No one had built a dome on this scale before, and Brunelleschi invented new construction techniques and equipment from his empirical knowledge of both Gothic and Roman architecture.

↓ Palazzo Medici, Florence, Italy, MICHELOZZO DI BARTOLOMMEO, 1444–59
The Medici, an aristocratic family of merchants and bankers who ruled Florence in the 15th century, introduced a completely new concept of urban living with this palazzo. Previously, urban oligarchies lived in sprawling agglomerations of buildings whose size and height proclaimed their power and prestige. The palazzo type was in many ways less practical, yet it provided an opportunity to show wealth and authority through knowledge of Classical and Humanist learning, rather than dimensions alone.

OTHER BUILDINGS

ITALY Loggia dei Lanzi, Florence, 1376–82; Baptistry doors, Florence, LORENZO GHIBERTI, 1401–24; Ospedale degli Innocenti, Florence, FILIPPO BRUNELLESCHI, 1419–24; Pazzi Chapel, Florence, FILIPPO BRUNELLESCHI, 1429–46; Santo Spirito, Florence, FILIPPO BRUNELLESCHI, 1445–82

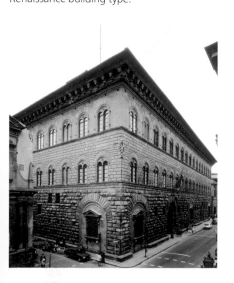

Structural Rationalism; Neoclassicism; Humanism; Idealism; Gothic Scholasticism

Medievalism; Baroque; Rococo

With numerous Roman remains to copy, Classical detail and form never entirely disappeared from Italian architecture, but the new focus on Classical scholarship during the Renaissance stimulated an almost archaeological attention to accuracy. Humanism interwove this interest with Neoplatonic thought, which privileged clear mathematical shapes and proportions. Architecture therefore became an intellectual as much as a practical discipline.

LEON BATTISTA ALBERTI (1404–72); *LUCIANO LAURANA* (1420–79); **DONATO BRAMANTE** (1444–1514)

Renaissance; Classicism; learning; scholarship; proportion; unity; Neoplatonism

Neoplatonic thought and Proto-Classical structures existed side by side for some time before Leon Battista Alberti brought the two strands together in his buildings and treatises, in particular *De Re Aedificatoria*. Showing his debt to the Classical world, Alberti valued civic virtue above all else. Architecture was a means of achieving and displaying it, thus it had to be accurate and, through an appreciation of

Neoplatonic thought expressed through precise mathematical order, able to carry sophisticated ideas about humans, society and their relationship to the divine. Alberti used Classical Orders and forms to establish hierarchies: the triumphal arch denoted an entrance to a church, while specific use of the various Orders could mark not just an important building, but also the relative status of its parts.

Florentine by birth, Alberti spent much of his life at the papal court and his ideas spread to many cities across northern Italy. Frederigo Montefeltro made his court at Urbino, one of the major centres of Humanist learning, in the late 15th century, employing the painter Piero della Francesca. His power of patronage helped to create the Ducale Palace, with Luciano Laurana's elegantly proportioned courtyard, and its art collection.

Born in Urbino in 1444, Donato Bramante grew up in a hotbed of Humanism. His buildings in Milan and Rome, where he commenced the rebuilding of St Peter's and completed the exquisite Tempietto, show the most refined synthesis of Classical learning and Neoplatonic thought.

KEY BUILDINGS

← Tempietto, Rome, Italy, DONATO BRAMANTE, 1502–10
Placed on what tradition held was the exact spot of St Peter's crucifixion, there was a practical reason for the size of this tiny church, and for its circular plan, which seems to address all directions equally. But this also followed the architectural ideals of designs based on Platonic forms, here expressed in the plan and hemispherical dome.

→ Palazzo Rucellai, Florence, Italy, LEON BATTISTA ALBERTI, 1446–57
Alberti introduced a new dimension to the palazzo design within a few years of the Palazzo Medici, by including Classical Orders in the facade, thus associating architect and client with the Humanist learning derived from the revival of Ancient Classical principles.

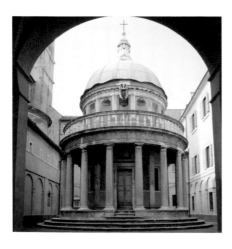

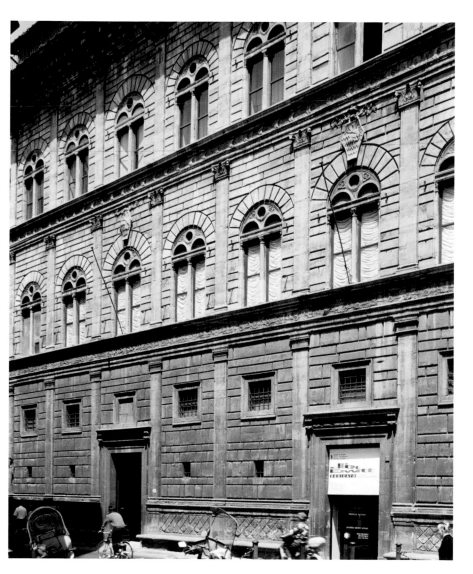

OTHER BUILDINGS
ITALY Palazzo Ducale, Urbino, LUCIANO LAURANA,
1444–82; Santa Maria Novella (facade), Florence, LEON
BATTISTA ALBERTI, 1456–70; San Sebastiano, Mantua,
LEON BATTISTA ALBERTI, 1459; Santa Maria delle
Grazie, Milan, DONATO BRAMANTE, 1492–7; Santa
Maria della Pace (cloister), Rome, DONATO BRAMANTE,
1500–04

 Idealism; Neoclassicism; Hellenic Classicism;
Roman Classicism

 Baroque; Rococo; Gothic Scholasticism

Renaissance architects sought to create perfection through the idealised synthesis of physical form and abstract ideas. This was difficult where they did not have total control of the setting, and virtually impossible when the new design adjoined an older one, especially where this was of Gothic design, which they considered barbaric. Very few had the opportunity to realise an 'ideal city', but almost all favoured free-standing, often centrally planned buildings.

ANTONIO FILARETE (c. 1400–69); **BERNARDO ROSSELLINO** (1409–64); **ANTONIO DA SANGALLO** (ELDER & YOUNGER, 1455–1534, 1485–1546); **GIULIANO DA SANGALLO** (1445–1516)

proportion; unity; centrality

Antonio Filarete's proposal for the ideal city of Sforzinda, was named after his patron Sforza, the Duke of Milan. The impractical nature of the town is shown in the tower of Vice and Virtue, with a brothel on the ground floor and an astronomical observatory on top.

Sforzinda was the first symmetrical town plan in the Renaissance, and set a precedent for numerous followers. One of the few to reach construction was Pienza, as Pope Pius II renamed his home village in southern Tuscany. Designed by Leon Battista Alberti's collaborator Bernardo Rossellino, a pair of palaces for the pope's family and the bishop flanks the cathedral around a symmetrical piazza. A city hall forms the fourth side. This suggests an ordered balance between religious, civic and private interests,

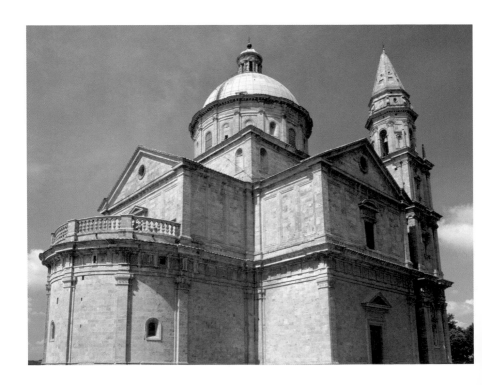

illustrating an idealised picture of the social structure. Cardinals were encouraged to build their own palaces along the main street, though the natural topography introduced a few curves to spoil its perfection. Pius's death in 1464 was a much more serious challenge to the ideals of Pienza. The cardinals returned to Rome leaving their palaces incomplete.

Though ideal cities were common in Renaissance architectural treatises, few were even started. For most architects, Idealism was embodied in individual buildings based on 'ideal' or Platonic forms that were believed to have a special connection to the divine, making them particularly suitable for churches in which the altar was placed in the centre. This clashed with liturgical practice, which required a long nave for the congregation who faced, but did not reach, the altar. The tension between longitudinal and centralised planning caused untold dilemmas, as demonstrated by the evolution of St Peter's in Rome, from Bramante's centralised plan, through numerous fluctuations to the compromise eventually realised.

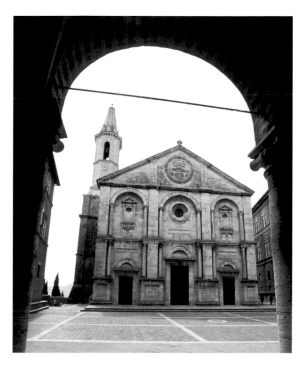

↑ Pienza, Italy, **BERNARDO ROSSELLINO**, 1458–64
Renaissance architectural ideals dictated urban design as much as individual buildings, and Pope Pius II transformed his home village into one of the most complete examples of an 'ideal city'. The cathedral, flanked by palazzi for the bishop and the pope's family, and facing a town hall, expresses the relationship between secular and religious power.

KEY BUILDINGS

Madonna di San Biagio, Montepulciano, Italy, ANTONIO DA SANGALLO (ELDER), 1519–29
Antonio da Sangallo made a compote of Platonic shapes in this church. Its plan is a Greek cross with four equal arms, one extended into a semi-circular apse, with a cylindrical drum surmounted by a hemispherical dome over the crossing (the junction between the nave and transepts). These pure forms are then given minimal Classical detail.

OTHER BUILDINGS

ITALY Santa Maria delle Carceri, Prato, GIULIANO DA SANGALLO, 1485; Palazzo della Cancelleria, ANON, Rome, 1486–96

 Humanism; Neoclassicism

 Baroque; Medievalism; Gothic Scholasticism

Mannerism

By the middle of the 16th century, it was clear that strict adherence to Renaissance precepts was not always possible, and that variations were necessary to meet practical contingencies. Mannerism is the way in which architects bent and adapted Classical precedents in form and detail, both for pragmatic reasons and for visual effect. It reorientated the chaste, intellectual and austere architecture of Humanism towards scenic effect and emotional response.

MICHELANGELO (1475–1564); BALDASSARE PERUZZI (1481–1536); MICHELE SANMICHELI (1484–1559); JACOPO SANSOVINO (1486–1570); GIULIO ROMANO (1499–1546); ANDREA PALLADIO (1508–80)

ornament; licence; illusion; inventive detailing

When Michelangelo became architect to St Peter's in Rome, in 1547 (see illustration on page 42) the clarity of Bramante's original vision had already been lost due to numerous half-finished reworkings. Michelangelo added a second square at 45 degrees to Bramante's plan, creating a dynamic composition that enabled him to incorporate the loose ends, and to create piers large enough to carry the huge drum and dome. In the drum he placed the long sides of oblong windows horizontally rather than vertically, and surmounted them with both a shell and an entablature – an example of the Mannerist practice of interweaving two compositional devices.

Mannerism made itself felt in many different ways. The Roman-born pupil of Raphael, Giulio Romano worked for the Gonzaga Dynasty in Mantua from the 1520s, introducing a series of departures from the Classical canon in his masterpiece the Palazzo del Te, in which rhythms alternate, pilasters mix with rustication, and arches with pediments. The extraordinary invention displays, but never departs from a broad conception of the Classical tradition, both literary and architectural, and culminates in a magnificent interior which though it has no architectural ornament, is covered with a painting depicting the giants overthrowing Classical order. Similarly, Andrea Palladio, who may have worked with Romano, expanded the Classical tradition to incorporate previously incompatible devices.

Illusion is also a key element in Baldassare Peruzzi's design for the Palazzo Massimo in Rome. Faced with the problem of an irregular site in which he had to squeeze a double palace for two brothers, he curved the facade to follow the street line. Behind is a series of illusions that are reinforced by the decorative scheme, inaugurating a principle that would reach its apogee in the Baroque period more than a century later.

KEY BUILDING
→ Basilica, Vicenza, Italy, ANDREA PALLADIO, 1546–9
Palladio's first public commission was to encase an existing hall within this two-storey arcade. Many of the dimensions were predetermined by the existing structure, and to fit these to his design Palladio superimposed various Classical devices – the essence of Mannerism – to give a flexibility that would not have been possible with a single order.

OTHER BUILDINGS
ITALY Biblioteca Laurentiana, Florence, MICHELANGELO, 1524; Capitol, Rome, MICHELANGELO, 1546; Palazzo del Te, Mantua, GIULIO ROMANO, 1525–35; Own House, Mantua, GIULIO ROMANO, 1544; Palazzo Massimo, Rome, BALDASSARE PERUZZI, 1532–6; Biblioteca San Marco, Venice, JACOPO SANSOVINO, 1536–53; Palazzo Thiene, Vicenza, ANDREA PALLADIO, 1542; Palazzo Chiericati, Vicenza, ANDREA PALLADIO, 1549; San Giorgio Maggiore, Venice, ANDREA PALLADIO, 1566; Il Redentore, Venice, ANDREA PALLADIO, 1576

Baroque; Rococo; Roman Classicism; Inventionism

Hellenic Classicism; Idealism; Rationalism

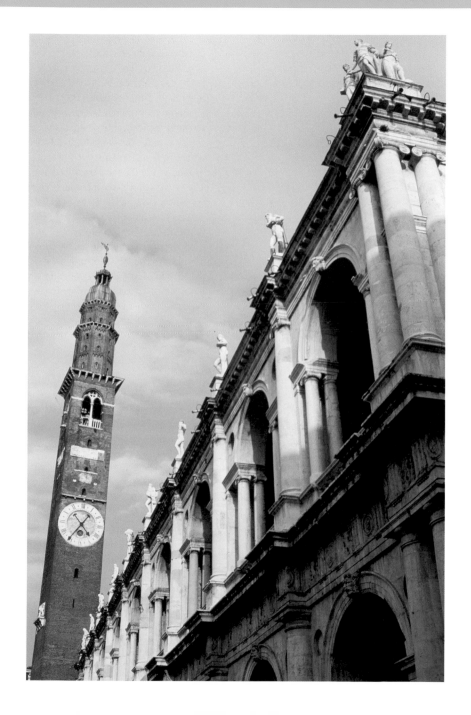

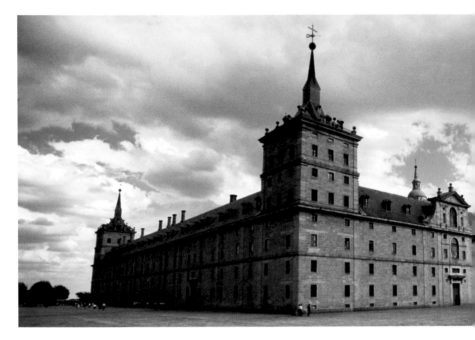

When faced in the mid-16th century with the dual challenge of the loss of much of its authority in Northern Europe following the Reformation, and the wish to incorporate Spanish and Portuguese colonies into its ambit, the Roman Catholic Church instituted a series of measures known as the Counter-Reformation. Pietism describes the influence of these measures on architecture, especially church design.

JACOPO VIGNOLA (1507–73);
JUAN BAUTISTA DE TOLEDO (d.1567);
CLAUDIO DE ARCINIEGA (1527–93); JUAN DE HERRARA (1530–97); GIACOMO DELLA PORTA (1537–1602); DOMENICO FONTANA (1543–1607); FRANCISCO BAUTISTA (1594–1679)

Counter-Reformation; doctrine

The reassertion of Roman Catholic doctrine in the mid-16th century created a demand for more churches and changed the nature of their design. New monastic orders like the Jesuits, founded to carry out missionary work and uphold the Counter-Reformation, needed new churches, while the Council of Trent codified doctrine and revived the ancient role of art as 'the Bible of the Illiterate'.

Painting and sculpture were to illustrate uplifting biblical stories, architecture to provide spaces to serve the new devotional patterns, resulting in a return to the medieval Latin-cross plan of a long nave, two transepts and an apse. Though this may have been rejected under the influence of Renaissance Neoplatonism, it gave the desired separation of clergy and laity, and the long nave provided plenty of space for side chapels devoted to individual saints. Unfortunately, not even the licence of Mannerism suggested a ready resolution to the old problem of designing Classical west fronts for essentially Gothic churches and, not surprisingly, initial attempts, such as Il

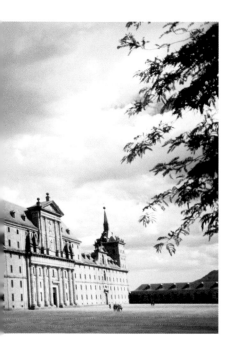

← El Escorial, near Madrid, Spain, JUAN BAUTISTA DE TOLEDO and JUAN DE HERRARA, 1559–84
This enormous complex including a palace, monastery, college and church, set in a bleak, mountainous location and built from a hard local granite that is hard to carve into ornament, captures the austerity that its psychologically tortured builder, Philip II, equated with piety. Its gridiron plan recalls the device on which his favourite saint, Lawrence, was roasted to death.

↓ Il Gesu, Rome, Italy, JACOPO VIGNOLA and GIACOMO DELLA PORTA, 1568–84
The Jesuit builders of this church were charged with reasserting Roman Catholic doctrine after the Protestant Reformation, a task that also called for inventive adaptations of Renaissance principles in church design. This attempt to unify the two lower aisles either side of a central nave in one unified composition was widely copied.

OTHER BUILDINGS
MEXICO Cathedral, Mexico City, CLAUDIO DE ARCINIEGO, 1585

ITALY Lateran Palace, Rome, DOMENICO FONTANA, 1586; San Giacomo degli Incurabili, Rome, FRANCESCO DA VOLTERRA, 1590; San Andrea della Valle, Rome, GIACOMO DELLA PORTA, 1591

 Baroque; Gothic Scholasticism; Christian Classicism

 Idealism; Humanism; Anglican Empiricism; Georgian Urbanism

Gesu, the Jesuits' mother church in Rome, were clumsy.

Spain, with its recently Muslim territories and significant Jewish population, felt the full political force of the Counter-Reformation. In architecture this led to the brutal insertion of a cathedral within the magnificent mosque at Cordoba, which even its instigator, Emperor Charles V, eventually regretted. Elsewhere in Spain, fecund decoration conveyed narrative messages and covered up volumetric awkwardness, though exceptions included El Escorial, Philip II's austerely sinister palace outside Madrid, whose gridiron plan was supposedly a permanent reminder of St Lawrence's agonising martyrdom.

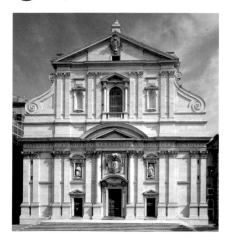

Printing meant that ideas could travel more quickly and effectively during the Renaissance than ever before, encouraging the writing, and facilitating the spread of treatises, one of the most important of which was by the Italian author Sebastiano Serlio. In the latter years of his life, Serlio also worked in France, and his ideas had certainly reached Britain by the end of the 16th century. Wherever the new ideas reached, they interacted with local conditions to create a wealth of regional variations.

SEBASTIANO SERLIO (1475–1554); DOMENICO DA CORTONA (1495–1549); PHILIBERT DE L'ORME (1510–70); ROBERT SMYTHSON (c.1536–1614); JOHN SMYTHSON (d. 1630); JOHN THORPE (1565–1655);; SIMON DE LA VALLEE (1590–1642); JACOB VAN CAMPEN (1595–1657); FRANCOIS MANSART (1598–1666)

adaptation; invention; printed treatises

Through the printed word, readers in France and England could gain an appreciation of Renaissance ideas decades before the architectural virtue of the period was recognised and the local construction industries could deliver it. Classical architecture first appeared in the details attached to buildings whose overall form was more traditional; for example, the chateaux of the Loire Valley or various collegiate buildings in Oxford or Cambridge. Later, Sebastiano Serlio attempted a practical demonstration of his treatises, several volumes of which were published in France in the 1540s and 1550s, in his design for Ancy-le-Franc. This introduced a new order and discipline to domestic building, though the local masons who altered it retained the steeply pitched roof and corner towers that were the hallmarks of French

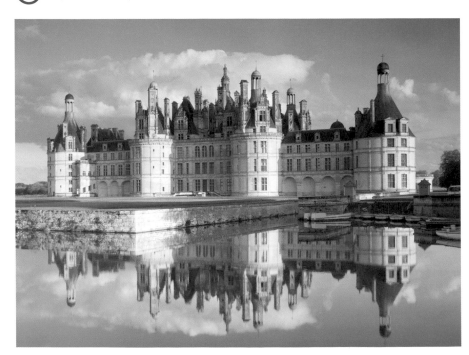

Regional Classicism

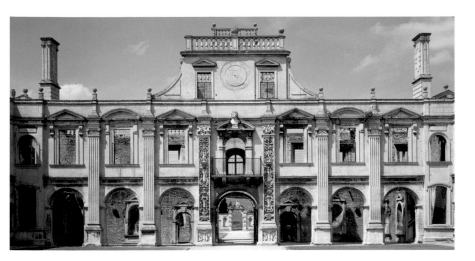

chateaux. In the hands of architects like Philibert de l'Orme, for example in his *hôtels* (town houses) for the rising class of administrators, these features slowly evolved into a coherent style.

A new elite made a similar contribution to English architecture, with the Elizabethan prodigy houses such as Longleat, Hardwick Hall and Burghley, in which the roofscapes turn chimneys and parapets into fragmentary columns and entablatures. No Italian architects of comparable status with Serlio worked in England, and responsibility for the design of these houses fell to masons such as Robert Smythson and John Thorpe. But underneath the vigorously and often inventively applied Classical detail, the plans were awkward resolutions of Renaissance symmetry with Medieval features like great halls, parlours and long galleries. Not until the following century did the full panoply of Renaissance Classicism reach England, and then it swept all before it.

The adoption of Classicism in other Northern European countries followed a similar pattern of iteration between local building practice and imported ideas.

KEY BUILDINGS

↑ Kirby Hall, Northamptonshire, England, THOMAS THORPE (attributed), 1570–72
Kirby is one of the 'prodigy houses' built by a new elite during Elizabeth I's reign, which synthesised Gothic tradition and Classicism. Kirby incorporates the sophistication of the giant (two-storey) pilasters first used by Michelangelo on the Capitol in Rome, but here they face an essentially Medieval plan.

← Chateau de Chambord, Loire Valley, France, DOMENICO DA CORTONA, 1519–47
A Classical energy seems to burst through the Medieval castle plan of the largest Loire chateau. There are Classical pilasters on the facade, while Renaissance details compete on the roofscape with traditional French turrets. Inside, a double spiral staircase shows the influence of Leonardo da Vinci, who lived nearby.

OTHER BUILDINGS

Ancy-le-Franc, Burgundy, France, SEBASTIANO SERLIO, c.1546; Chateau d'Anet, Loire Valley, France, PHILIBERT DE L'ORME, 1548; Palais de Fontainebleu, Seine-et-Marne, France, GILLES LE BRETON, 1568; Hardwick Hall, Derbyshire, England, ROBERT SMYTHSON, 1590–7; Maritzhuis, the Hague, The Netherlands, JACOB VAN CAMPEN, 1633–5; House of Nobles, Stockholm, Sweden, SIMON DE LA VALLEE, 1641–74

Mannerism; Anglican Empiricism; Baroque

Idealism; Humanism; Neoclassicism

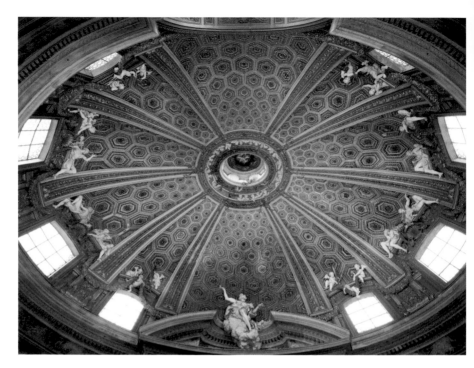

With Baroque, Classical architects made a decisive break with Renaissance Humanism and Idealism. Baroque forms were richer and more varied, stressing illusion and spectacle rather than the embodiment of pure ideals in Platonic forms, originating from a desire to reinforce religious doctrine. However, the ability of Baroque to convey non-architectural ideas brought it into contact with wide-ranging concepts from mathematical discovery to political Absolutism.

GIANLORENZO BERNINI (1598–1680); FRANCESCO BORROMINI (1599–1667); PIETRO DA CORTONA (1596–1669); BALDASSARE LONGHENA (1598–1682); CARLO RAINALDI (1611–91); GUARINO GUARINI (1624–83); FILIPPO JUVARRA (1678–1736)

complexity; movement; emotion; illusion; suspense

Baroque architecture was born out of two great Roman architects of the 17th century: Gianlorenzo Bernini and Francesco Borromini. Both created free-flowing and complex forms, assimilating into the Classical tradition political, liturgical and topographical realities that Renaissance ideals of 'pure' forms and free-standing buildings found hard to absorb.

Following Baroque painters like Caravaggio, and trained as a sculptor, Bernini used gesture and posture to convey human emotions invoked by particular situations. He often combined sculptural figures and sometimes painting to personalise and add explicit narrative to architectural effects; for example, in Rome's San Andrea al Quirinale, in the depiction of St Andrew's soul leaving his crucified body and ascending, assisted by *putti* (young boys), to the heavenly light of a lantern atop a dome. Even the Colonnade of the Piazza San Pietro resembles arms enfolding and gathering humanity into religious orthodoxy, an essential aim of the Counter-Reformation.

Borromini's sources were more abstract, but combined for equally compelling effect. He drew on his knowledge of stonework (from his family's masons yards) and infused this with a deep understanding of geometry to create extraordinarily complex forms. His masterpiece, San Carlo alle Quattro Fontane, achieves a wonderfully dynamic unity of triangles and circles, interweaving symbols of the Trinity with the unity and all-pervading power of Christ's church.

Baroque spread throughout the Catholic world and had some effect outside, notably on Anglican Empiricism. But away from Rome it was its decorative aspects rather than its spatial and structural inventiveness that dominated. One exception was in Turin, where Guarino Guarini and, later, Filippo Juvarra created works that rival those of Borromini in their complex Rationalism. A distinguished mathematician and philosopher, Guarini's knowledge underlies his architecture. Advanced thinking, he showed, could increase the expressive potential of architecture beyond conventional stylistic canons.

KEY BUILDINGS
San Andrea al Quirinale, Rome, Italy, GIANLORENZO BERNINI, 1658–70
Bernini's church for the Jesuit noviciate is the epitome of the Baroque synthesis between architecture, sculpture and painting to create an overwhelming visual effect. A painting behind the altar depicts the martyrdom of St Andrew (Andrea). His soul rises through a broken pediment above, assisted by the upward gesture of the angelic figure, ascending to the heavenly dome and lantern.

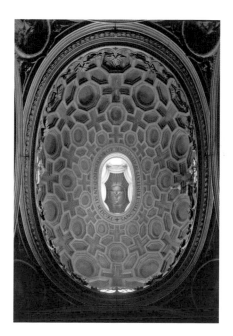

↑ San Carlo alle Quattro Fontane, Rome, FRANCESCO BORROMINI, 1633–67
Borromini achieved a Baroque complexity through overlapping architectural compositions, rather than the integration of different artistic media. The interior is derived from a plan that combines a triangle, circle and oval, each having symbolic resonance, and unified under an elliptical dome.

OTHER BUILDINGS
ITALY Sant Ivo della Sapienza, Rome, FRANCESCO BORROMINI,1642–60; Piazza San Pietro, Rome, GIANLORENZO BERNINI, 1656; Santa Maria della Pace (west front and piazza), Rome, PIETRO DA CORTONA, 1656–7; Santa Maria dei Miracoli/Santa Maria in Monte Santo, Piazza del Popolo, Rome, CARLO RAINALDI, 1662; Palazzo Rezzonico, Venice, BALDASSARE LONGHENA, 1667; Palazzo Carignano, Turin, GUARINO GUARINI, 1679; Superga Temple, Turin, FILIPPO JUVARRA, 1715–27

Rococo; Sublimism; Gothic Scholasticism; Mannerism

Idealism; Neoclassicism; Rationalism

Absolutism describes the architecture of the powerful European rulers who created the Absolute states of the 17th and 18th centuries. In politics they drew on Renaissance statecraft which the 19th-century historian Jacob Burckhardt termed 'the state as a work of art'. This meant that every aspect of statecraft was subject to rational examination, and pinpointing the close affinity between art, architecture and politics. Absolutist architecture shows a comparable development of principles taken from the Renaissance.

LOUIS LE VAU (1612–70); CLAUDE PERRAULT (1613–88); JOHANN FISCHER VON ERLACH (1656–1723); JACQUES-ANGE GABRIEL (1698–1782); BARTOLOMEO RASTRELLI (1700–71); LUIGI VANVITELLI (1700–73)

power; monarchy; centralised control; divine right; authority

In Absolutism, whether in architecture or statecraft, everything revolved around the reigning monarch. The Renaissance had already shown the potential of centrally planned buildings, and Mannerism and the Baroque had introduced a degree of licence that helped to reinforce programmatic ideas. However, Absolutism appropriated the idea of a central focus, reinforced its symmetry with radial devices, mixed it with Baroque scenography and presented it on vast scale. Its greatest single monument is Versailles, from where Louis XIV really could believe that he was the Sun King, as the trees and fountains of the park seemed to bow to his will as subserviently as his obsequious courtiers. Even the roads from Paris converged at its entrance courtyard, as if the capital and country led only to the king's feet.

Versailles owes much to the chateau of Vaux-le-Vicomte. Though much smaller, it too radiates from a single source across an extensive formal park. The grandiose building plans of its creator, Nicolas Fouquet, aroused the suspicion of Louis XIV, and Fouquet was condemned to life imprisonment, confirming the king's absolute power.

Absolute rulers and their architects realised that vast scale could be made even more impressive using visual tricks of composition and perspective. Thus the entire town of Karlsruhe in Germany radiates outwards from its ducal palace almost to the limits of the state itself. Larger countries could not be reduced to single cities, but Johann Fischer von Erlach implied that Vienna was the successor to Rome and Constantinople in his design for the Karlskirche, while Peter the Great of Russia founded an entire city, St Petersburg, in an attempt to drag the whole of Russia into the

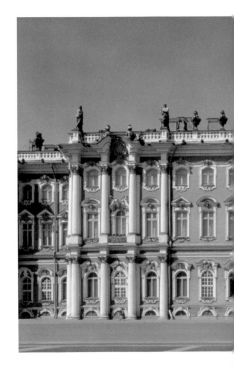

modern world under his unchallenged leadership, an achievement cemented by his formidable successor Catherine the Great.

KEY BUILDINGS

Chateau de Versailles, Paris, France, CHARLES LE BRUN, 1661–78
Louis XIV, the 'Sun King' and Europe's most powerful monarch, expanded a relatively small chateau in two phases in the 1660s and 1670s. Its unprecedented scale stretched architectural ingenuity in creating a unified composition for the 1,320-foot facade, but the symbolism of placing the king's bedroom at the centre, and the park radiating away from it, is obvious.

Winter Palace, St Petersburg, Russia, BARTOLOMEO RASTRELLI, 1754–62
The whole of St Petersburg is a monument to Russian tsarism, one of the most extreme and longest lasting of the European Absolute monarchies, and the Winter Palace is its symbolic and physical heart. Built for the Tsarina Elizabeth, whose father Peter the Great founded the city, it is vast, floridly decorated and contains magnificent interiors designed to impress.

OTHER BUILDINGS

East Front, Louvre, Paris, France, CLAUDE PERRAULT, 1667; Karlskirche, Vienna, Austria, JOHANN FISCHER VON ERLACH, 1716; Tsarskoe Selo, St Petersburg, Russia, BARTOLOMEO RASTRELLI, 1749–56; Royal Palace, Caserta, Italy, LUIGI VANVITELLI, 1751; Place de le Concord, Paris, JACQUES-ANGE GABRIEL, 1755

 Rococo; Pre-Classicism; Sublimism

 Rationalism; Functionalism; Exoticism

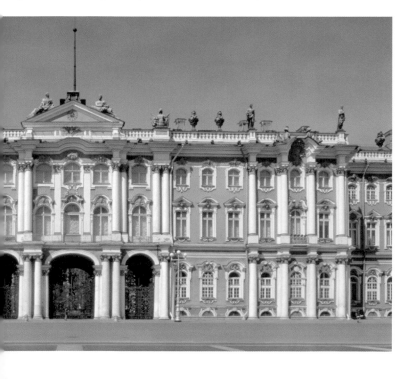

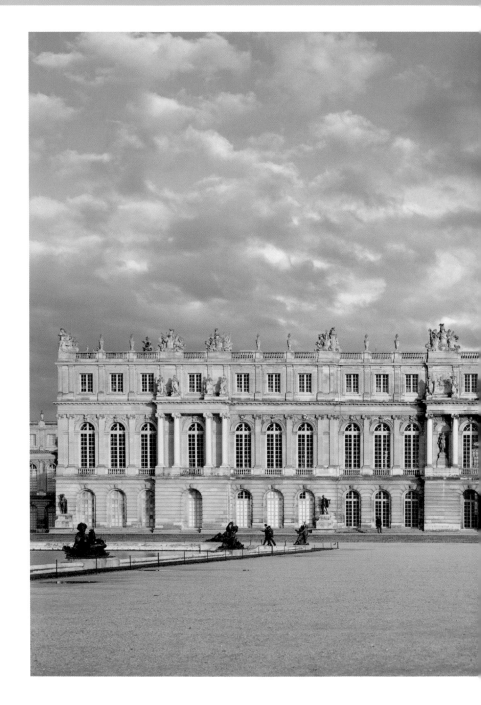

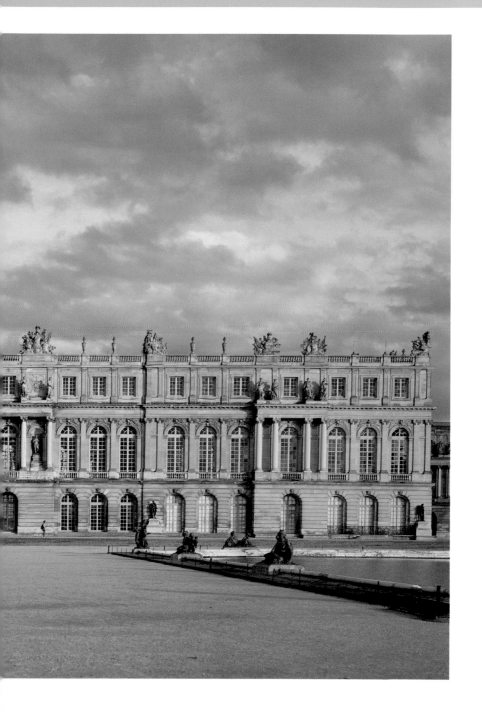

Anglican Empiricism is an inventive and richly decorated version of Classicism that emerged in England at the end of the 17th century. In adapting the Classical language to practical and political ends, it has some affinity with Baroque. However, where Baroque asserted Roman Catholic doctrine and merged easily into Absolutism, Anglican Empiricism was formed around the re-established Church of England, as new aristocratic oligarchy became the dominant political force and scientific discoveries overturned established beliefs.

JOHN WEBB (1611–72); ROGER PRATT (1620–84); CHRISTOPHER WREN (1632–1723); NICHOLAS HAWKSMOOR (1661–1736); JOHN VANBRUGH (1664–1726); JAMES GIBBS (1682–1754)

new learning; scientific inquiry; experiment; calculate; geometry; pragmatism

By the Restoration of the English monarchy in 1660, both the intellectual climate and the structure of patronage had changed radically since Inigo Jones had introduced Renaissance Classicism to Britain half a century earlier. This is

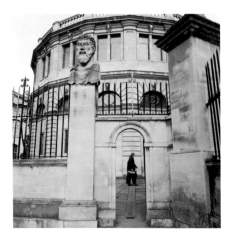

illustrated in the career of Sir Christopher Wren, a university-educated scientist whose knowledge and social position allowed him to tackle the challenges of building the new social order.

Both of Wren's first buildings – Pembroke College Cambridge, where his uncle the Bishop of Ely paid for a new chapel, and the Sheldonian Theatre Oxford, where he was professor of astronomy – were the products of his Royalist, ecclesiastical and academic connections. In the latter he used his mathematical knowledge to span the space without resorting either to Gothic vaulting or intermediate columns. His career received an enormous boost after the Great Fire of London in 1666, though neither his ambitious city plan nor his preferred 'Great Model' design for St Paul's Cathedral were were ever realised. However, the numerous churches he designed show extraordinary inventiveness in meeting Anglican liturgical needs on sites that are often small and awkwardly shaped.

As surveyor-general of the King's Works for almost 50 years from 1669, Wren had great influence over architectural practice as it began to acquire an intellectual strain, through his own work and that of his fellow Royal Society members, such as Robert Hooke and John Evelyn. His collaborators in the Office of Works included Nicholas Hawksmoor, a mason by training who brought practical building knowledge to Wren's intellectual ideas, and Sir John Vanbrugh, the playwright, wit and one-time Bastille prisoner who also designed the most spectacular English country houses Blenheim Palace and Castle Howard. Their bold and exuberant licence with Classicism earned them the ire of the Palladians who revolutionised English taste in the early 18th century.

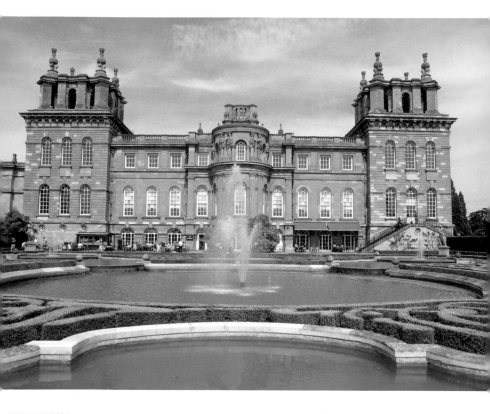

KEY BUILDINGS

Sheldonian Theatre, Oxford, England,
SIR CHRISTOPHER WREN, 1664–9
Wren used his ability as a mathematician, which he
developed whilst a professor at Oxford, to reinforce the
Classical feel of a Roman amphitheatre for the
university's academic assembly hall. He devised a grid of
relatively flat timber trusses spanning the 70-foot space
without Gothic vaulting or intermediate columns, both
of which would have ruined the desired effect.

Blenheim Palace, Woodstock, Oxon, England,
JOHN VANBRUGH, 1705–20
Britain's grandest country house was designed by an
individual with no architectural training. Vanbrugh
picked up ideas from his varied experience as wit,
playwright and soldier, as well as clients from his Whig
connections. He composed his designs with a flair and
power that belies their pattern-book origins.
Construction problems were resolved by Nicholas
Hawksmoor.

OTHER BUILDINGS

UK St Stephen Walbrook, London, CHRISTOPHER
WREN, 1672–87; Greenwich Naval College, London,
CHRISTOPHER WREN (with JOHN WEBB), 1696–1715; St
Mary Woolnoth, London, NICHOLAS HAWKSMOOR,
1716–27; Christchurch Spitalfields, London,
NICHOLAS HAWKSMOOR, 1723–9; St Martin in the
Fields, London, JAMES GIBB, 1722–6

Inventionism;
Georgian Urbanism

Neoclassicism;
Rococo

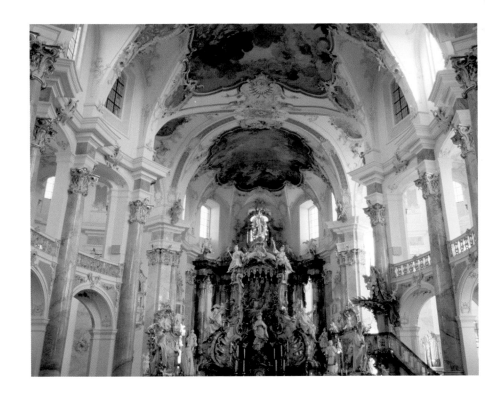

Rococo extends the richness of ornament and free-flowing forms, introduced to the Classical language by Baroque architects to even greater heights of illusion and sensory stimulation. Closely associated with the Roman Catholic world and, in particular, the Holy Roman Empire and southern Germany, it emphasises the mysterious and intuitive aspects of belief, and gave rise to numerous churches, monasteries and palaces for electors and other rulers.

JAKOB PRANDTAUER (1660–1726); GERMAIN BOFFRAND (1667–1754); BALTHASAR NEUMANN (1687–1753); MATHAÜS PÖPPELMANN (1662–1736); LUKAS VON HILDEBRANDT (1668–1745); JOHANN DIENTZENHOFER (1689–1751); JOHANN MICHAEL FISCHER (1692–1766); GIUSEPPE GALLI DA BIBIENA (1696–1757)

complexity; lightness; illusion; restlessness; decoration

At its best, Rococo combines the abstraction of architectural principles based on form and geometry, with the narrative effect of lavish pictorial ornament. Balthasar Neumann, whose pilgrimage church at Vierzehnheiligen in Bavaria is the apotheosis of the Rococo period, began his career as a military engineer, until his employer, the Prince-Bishop of Würzburg, sent him to Vienna and Paris to study architecture. Where most of his contemporaries in southern Germany during the early 18th century understood the basics of traditional building craft and created their effects primarily through florid decoration,

Neumann instead brought an understanding of architectural principles. At Vierzehnheiligen he composed an extraordinarily sophisticated plan of overlapping shapes and flowing volumes where space, form and light combine with decoration to underpin the sensory impression with intellectual rigour.

The primary aim of Rococo architects, in an age when scepticism and schism undermined the authority of the Catholic Church, was to provide an overwhelming experience through sculptural and painterly effects that reinforced Catholic doctrine. However, Rococo's potential to impress also appealed to secular rulers across the Holy Roman Empire, from the petty princelings to the emperor himself. Elector August the Strong of Saxony commissioned the Zwinger Palace in Dresden as a setting for pageants, but such is the richness of decoration, with ornamental device ladled upon ornamental device, that it creates an air of fantasy and restlessness irrespective of any festivities that may have taken place there.

By stressing scenography over construction, and in its association with noble authority and Catholic mysticism, Rococo represents a concept of architecture that stands in complete contrast to the line of development that extends from Neoclassicism through Structural Rationalism into Modernism.

Zwinger Palace, Dresden, Germany, MATHAÜS PÖPPELMANN, 1711–22
The Zwinger's ornate architecture gives away its function as a setting for spectacles. It was built for the Elector of Saxony, August the Strong and, though full of Classical details, they are combined with a distinctly un-Classical exuberance that refers more to the hedonistic tastes of its princely patron.

OTHER BUILDINGS
AUSTRIA Melk Monastery, JAKOB PRANDTAUER, 1702–14; Belvedere, Vienna, LUKAS VON HILDEBRANDT, 1714–23

FRANCE Hotel de Soubise, Paris, GERMAIN BOUFFRAND, 1737–40

GERMANY Pommersfelden Schloss, JOHANN DIENTZENHOFER, from 1711; Ottobeuren Abbey, JOHANN MICHAEL FISCHER, 1744–67; Opera House, Bayreuth, GIUSEPPE GALLI DA BIBIENA, 1747–53

 Decorative Industrialism; Baroque

Neoclassicism; Humanism; Idealism

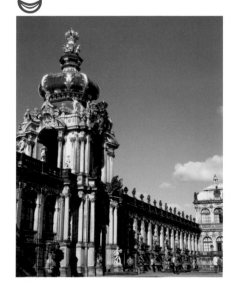

KEY BUILDINGS
Vierzehnheiligen, Bavaria, Germany, BALTHASAR NEUMANN, 1743–72
The exterior of this pilgrimage church gives away little of its riotous interior. Behind the undulating west front is a nave based on two ovals (the second with the altar of 14 saints), a pair of circular transepts and another oval for the choir, all embellished with elaborate decoration that complements the competing solid and spatial geometries.

A taste for the architecture of Andrea Palladio came to England via Inigo Jones, who met the Mannerist master's ageing assistant Vicenzo Scamozzi during his visits to Italy in the early 1600s. A century later, Lord Burlington and fellow architects adapted Palladian principles to the English climate and social conditions. Through them, Palladio and Palladianism became the inspiration for the great period of English country-house building in the 18th century.

COLEN CAMPBELL (1673–1729); WILLIAM KENT (1685–1748); LORD BURLINGTON (1694–1753); HENRY FLITCROFT (1697–1769); THOMAS JEFFERSON (1743–1826); HENRY HOLLAND (1745–1806)

Palladio; symmetry; proportion; Arcadia

In 1715, Colen Campbell published *Vitruvius Britannicus,* a rallying cry against what were seen as the excesses of architects like Wren, Hawksmoor and Vanbrugh. In Lord Burlington, a wealthy 21-year-old aristocrat with artistic tastes, and fresh from a recent visit to Italy, the nascent movement found an individual who had not only the means to put their ideas into practice, but also the capability to make a substantial contribution to them.

Burlington assembled his artistic protégés to remodel his town house on Piccadilly in London, though the final result owes at least as much to his own vision as to any other individual. He quickly tired of Campbell's rigidity, and gave greater responsibility to William Kent who, though originally a painter, was to prosper as an architect under Burlington's patronage and tutelage. But it was Palladio who Burlington's circle most admired. Burlington himself made a second visit to Italy specifically to study his work, which resulted in his villa at Chiswick that is closely based on Palladio's Villa Rotunda.

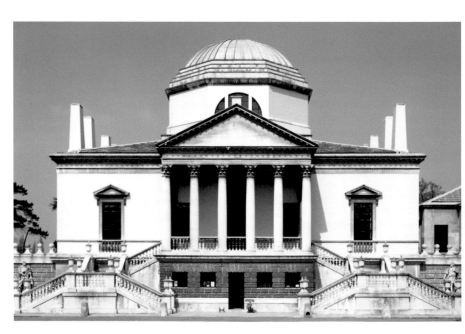

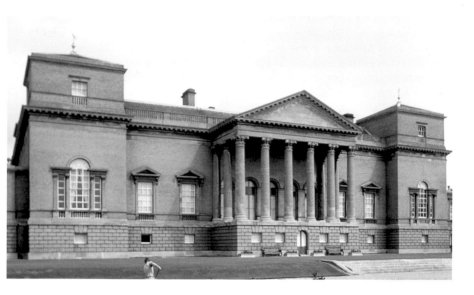

Burlington was inspired by the principles of Classical composition, symmetry and detail rather than exact copies. With their relatively small central blocks and extensive wings, Palladio's villas on the Venetian mainland also suited the lifestyles, ambitions and means of England's landowners, while his town palaces and churches suggested various models for town houses and institutions. From the grandiose, such as Wanstead, Stourhead and Houghton Hall for Prime Minister Walpole, to the relatively modest, Palladio's influence mediated by Burlington and his associates touched all aspects of British architecture, also reaching the US and distant Russia.

KEY BUILDINGS
Chiswick House, London, England,
LORD BURLINGTON, 1725–9
Lord Burlington called the house he designed for himself a villa, and used it to demonstrate his knowledge and mastery of principles derived from Andrea Palladio, whose Villa Rotunda is the closest model. But in conjuring up a variety of room shapes, and introducing windows just below the dome to light the central areas Burlington adapted them to English circumstances.

↑ Holkham Hall, Norfolk, England, WILLIAM KENT, from 1734
Kent started his career as a painter under the patronage of Lord Burlington, whose influence pervades one of the grandest English Palladian country houses. Here, Palladian motifs, the rusticated basement, Corinthian portico and windows with two flat lintels either side of an arch are adapted to the seat of a great English magnate, Lord Leicester.

OTHER BUILDINGS
UK Burlington House (the Royal Academy), London, COLEN CAMPBELL, WILLIAM KENT, LORD BURLINGTON et al, from 1717; Mereworth Castle, Kent, COLEN CAMPBELL, 1722–5; Stourhead, Wiltshire, COLEN CAMPBELL, 1721–4; Dormitory, Westminster School, London, LORD BURLINGTON, 1722–30

US Monticello, Virginia, THOMAS JEFFERSON, 1769–1809

 Idealism; Mannerism; Neoclassicism

 Baroque; Rococo; Medievalism

In the 18th century, London, Edinburgh and Bath redefined the scope of Classical town planning. Working on a large scale and under the constraints of speculative development, architects extended the repertoire of streets, squares and crescents to bring a sense of Classical grandeur and hierarchy to new urban quarters. Even though individual buildings were often simply built, with minimal decoration, their position within an overall ensemble meant they still conveyed an impression of Classicism, but adapted to local economic and topographical conditions.

INIGO JONES (1573–1652); **GEORGE DANCE** (ELDER & YOUNGER, 1695–1768, 1741–1825); **JOHN WOOD** (ELDER & YOUNGER, 1704–54, 1728–81); **ROBERT ADAM** (1728–92); **THOMAS LEVERTON** (1743–1824); **JOHN NASH** (1752–1835)

speculative development; adaptation; craft; economy

Inigo Jones and his client the Earl of Bedford brought Renaissance town planning to London in the 1630s, in the form of the Covent Garden Piazza. Inspired by his visits to Italy, and witnessing the Place Royale in Paris under construction in 1609, Jones designed a regular, arcaded piazza ringed by houses, with St Paul's Church at one end. This served as a precedent when London's expansion began in earnest after the political upheavals of the mid-17th century.

The great innovation at the time was to divide land into narrow plots for individual houses. These could be sold singly or in small groups on leases that obliged the purchaser to build a house that would revert to the landowner, typically 99 years later. Wealthy families such as the Russells (the Dukes of Bedford) and Grosvenors, who owned land on the fringe of a rapidly expanding London, followed this course from the 1720s

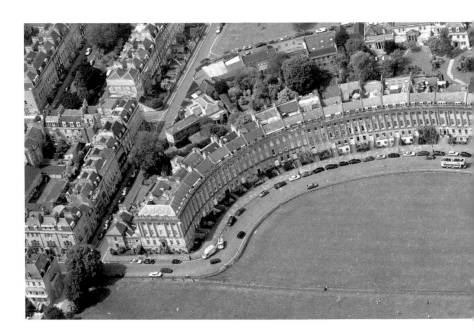

onwards, ensuring that the layout and quality of building would keep their estates attractive and valuable.

Moving to Bath from London in 1727, John Wood the Elder commenced the sequence of Queen Square, the Circus and Royal Crescent that his son John completed nearly 50 years later. Skilfully composed facades derived from Classical precedents disguise the fact that behind are individual houses rather than a nobleman's palace. As clerk of works to the City of London in 1767, George Dance Junior used the circus form in particular to integrate busy traffic arteries within monumental set pieces, and by 1800 crescents and circuses had become part of the repertoire of town planning from Bristol to Edinburgh New Town, while the Adam brothers developed the idea of unifying diverse buildings behind a single facade in their schemes for Fitzroy Square and the Adelphi in London.

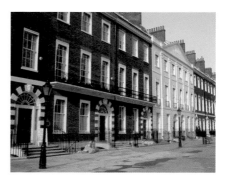

KEY BUILDINGS

↑ Bedford Square, London, England, THOMAS LEVERTON, 1775
London expanded rapidly in the 18th century as landowners began to develop estates on the city's fringes. Most of these estates followed the pattern of laying out land as streets and squares and selling off plots to individual builders who accepted conditions that ensured a degree of homogeneity. Bedford Square is on land owned by the Dukes of Bedford.

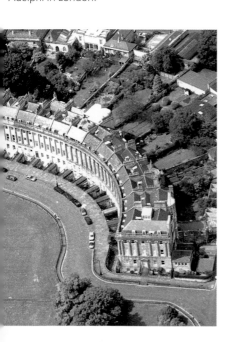

← Royal Crescent, Bath, England, JOHN WOOD (YOUNGER), 1767–71
In the 18th century, British architects looked to Ancient Rome for precedents to design new urban quarters. The Royal Crescent is loosely based on the Colosseum, adapted to housing for residents in the fashionable spa. A giant order of Ionic half-columns brings out its inherent grandeur, but its otherwise sparse ornament betrays that, like almost all Georgian town planning, this was a speculative development.

OTHER BUILDINGS
UK Edinburgh New Town, VARIOUS ARCHITECTS, from 1767; Covent Garden Piazza, London, INIGO JONES, 1631; The Minories, City of London, GEORGE DANCE (YOUNGER), 1765–70; St George's Circus, Southwark, London, GEORGE DANCE (YOUNGER), 1785–1820; The Adelphi, London, ROBERT ADAM AND BROTHERS, 1768–72; Regent Street and Regent's Park, London, JOHN NASH, from 1811

Anglican Empiricism; Neoclassicism; Regional Classicism; Roman Classicism

Anti-Urbanism; Pietism; Victorianism

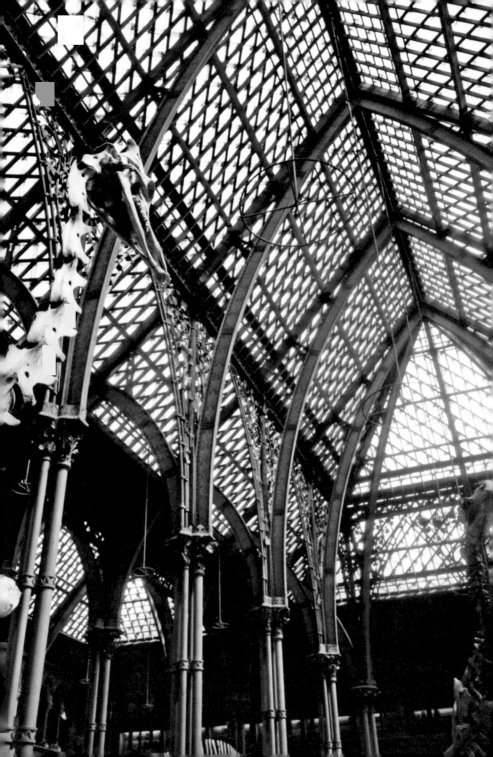

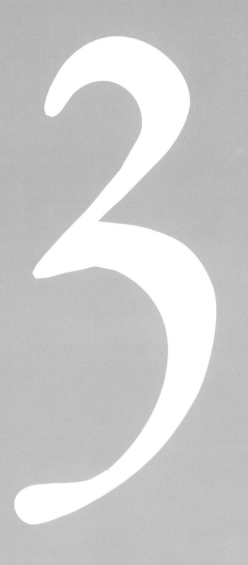

EARLY MODERN

Neoclassicism

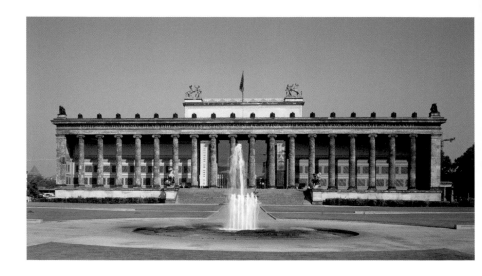

Neoclassicism arose out of a belief that architectural movements like Baroque and Rococo took architecture too far from its origins, and a consequent interest in discovering what its origins were. Rational thought, derived from the prevailing intellectual climate of the Enlightenment, and archaeological discoveries, both helped this quest.

MARC-ANTOINE LAUGIER (1713–69); JACQUES-GERMAIN SOUFFLOT (1713–80); JACQUES GONDOIN (1737–1818); THOMAS JEFFERSON (1743–1826); PIERRE VIGNON (1762–1828); BENJAMIN LATROBE (1764–1820); KARL FRIEDRICH SCHINKEL (1780–1841); ROBERT SMIRKE (1781–1867); LEO VON KLENZE (1784–1864)

restraint; order; form; discipline; reason; Enlightenment

Superficially, Neoclassicism sprang from the new knowledge of ancient architecture that came from archaeological discoveries in centres of Classical antiquity. However, there was also an important theoretical dimension. All architecture, argued Marc-Antoine Laugier in his *Essai sur*

l'*Architecture* of 1753, could be derived from the 'primitive hut', the 'noble savage's' rational response to the need for shelter comprising a simple structure of four tree trunks for columns, and branches for a pitched roof. These elements were organised into the basic forms of squares and triangles, reflecting the belief that reason and natural forms have the same root.

This intellectual conceit was an appealing alternative to Rococo and owed much to Vitruvius's description of the mythical origins of architecture, but it went far beyond a revival of antique forms. Ultimately, it gave architecture a conceptual model that replaced the dependence on stylistic traditions with connections to reason and attempts to order society along Rational lines. Thus Neoclassicism helped to lay the foundations for Structural Rationalism and, later, architectural Modernism.

By asserting the primacy of columns rather than piers and pilasters, and unbroken entablatures rather than arches, Jacques-Germain Soufflot's design for the church of Paris's patron saint, Sainte

Geneviève (later the Pantheon), started in 1754, demonstrates Laugier's influence. This disciplined architecture sprang from the French Enlightenment and inspired many designs where such ideas held sway. It was the obvious choice for the growing number of museums of Classical antiquities, from Sir Robert Smirke's pedantic interpretation in the British Museum to Karl Friedrich Schinkel's more elegant and refined Altes Museum in Berlin. The Classical scholar-turned-Neoclassical architect William Wilkins adopted it for the secular and rational foundation of University College, London, while Benjamin Latrobe took it to the US.

KEY BUILDINGS
Altes Museum, Berlin, Germany,
KARL FRIEDRICH SCHINKEL, 1824–8
The colonnade of giant Ionic columns that greets visitors shows Schinkel's austere and rigorous interpretation of Classicism. Greek architecture stood for a combination of culture and discipline, which he adapted here to the new function of a museum, and generally to serve the ambitions of Prussia to turn Berlin into an 'Athens of the North'.

Panthéon (formerly Sainte Geneviève), Paris, France, JACQUES-GERMAIN SOUFFLOT, from 1756
Soufflot's design for a church for the patron saint of Paris is a Neoclassical version of the formula for giant cathedrals of great domes above vast naves. Previous examples had carried the dome's weight on clumsy walls and piers. Soufflot intended the structure to be columns and an entablature, turning the interior into a forest of Classical features.

OTHER BUILDINGS
School of Surgery, Paris, France, JACQUES GONDOIN, 1769–75; The White House, Washington DC, US, JAMES HOBAN and BENJAMIN LATROBE, 1792–1829; Baltimore Cathedral, Maryland, US, BENJAMIN LATROBE, 1804–18 ; La Madeleine, Paris, PIERRE VIGNON, 1806; Glyptothek, Munich, Germany, LEO VON KLENZE, 1816–34; University of Virginia, Charlottesville, Virginia, US, THOMAS JEFFERSON, 1817–26; British Museum, London, England, ROBERT SMIRKE, 1823–47

 Hellenic Classicism; Humanism; Idealism; Palladianism; Neo-Rationalism

 Baroque; Rococo; Medievalism; Victorianism

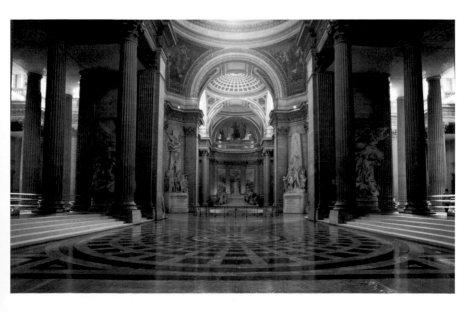

Deliberately contrived asymmetry and picturesque composition allowed architects to introduce new visual effects and suggest different relationships with nature than those possible in the Classical tradition. Immediate precedents came from landscape painters like Claude Lorrain as well as literary sources; however, an interest in non-Classical architecture led some architects to begin looking at Gothic, Indian and Chinese buildings.

WILLIAM CHAMBERS (1723–96); **JAMES WYATT** (1747–1813); **JOHN NASH** (1752–1835); **SAMUEL PEPYS COCKERELL** (1754–1827)

orientalism; picturesque; sensation; titillation; restlessness

Irregular scenes where nature seemed to dominate over intellect excited pleasurable sensations, so argued the picturesque theorists Richard Payne Knight and Uvedale Price at the end of the 18th century. Their ideas brought an intellectual dimension to existing trends in landscape design, which was already experimenting with irregularity and exotic influences from the Far East. With Kew Gardens' Pagoda and the China Pavilion in the grounds of the Swedish Royal Palace at Drottningholm, both completed in the 1760s, oriental forms had taken their place alongside sham ruins in gardens and parks. Informality even managed to creep into France, at Marie Antoinette's whimsically pastoral village, Petit Trianon, on the Versailles estate.

What excited architects about these new ideas was the scope they offered to depart from, or contrast with academic Classicism, opening the door to an entirely new range of visual effects. John Nash first explored the possibilities of asymmetrical composition and Gothic detailing before transforming Brighton's Royal Pavilion (1815–23) for the Prince Regent into an oriental fantasy. Even his Regent's Park, though outwardly

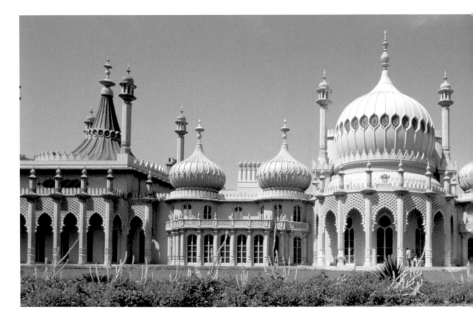

Classical, is strongly scenographic. Along with Samuel Pepys Cockerell's Indian-derived Sezincote for a retired nabob, the Royal Pavilion shows how such architectural styles changed from a public display of intellectual and social status to a way of satisfying private fancies. Though later applications of such styles strove for greater accuracy, the association of particular styles with particular sets of values persisted.

KEY BUILDINGS

Royal Pavilion, Brighton, England, JOHN NASH, 1815–23

Where Chambers strove for accuracy to his original models, Nash used architectural styles as the basis to create spectacular visual effects. He had no qualms about mixing or inventing details. His aim was to conjure illusion and play to the emotions and senses rather than scholarship or intellect.

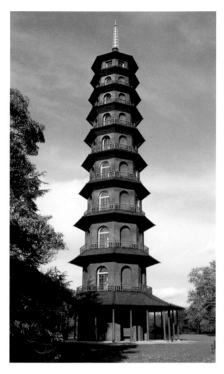

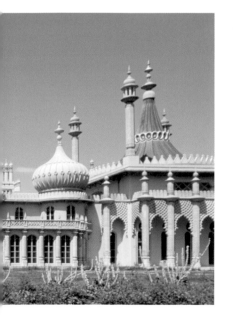

↑ **Pagoda, Kew Gardens, London, England, WILLIAM CHAMBERS, 1757–62**

A taste for Chinese decoration swept across Europe in the 18th century as trade with Asia increased. Chambers was one of very few European architects who had been to China. The idea here was to grace the gardens of a royal palace with an exotic form from outside of Western tradition. But in this project, Chambers strove unsuccessfully for the same degree of archaeological accuracy that marked his Classical designs.

OTHER BUILDINGS

China Pavilion, Drottningholm, Sweden, CARL JOHAN CRONSTEDT and CARL FREDRIK ADELCRANTZ, 1760; Sezincote, Gloucestershire, England, SAMUEL PEPYS COCKERELL, 1803–15; Ashbridge House, Hertfordshire, England, JAMES WYATT, from 1808

 Rococo; Expressionism; Postmodernism

 Neoclassicism; Rationalism; Palladianism

During the 18th century the emerging discipline of aesthetics began to question the conventional meanings and associations of traditional architectural styles and forms. But in exploring how art creates sensory and intellectual impressions, aesthetics also increased architecture's expressive possibilities. Sublimism exploited these new opportunities.

ETIENNE-LOUIS BOULLÉE (1728–99); CLAUDE-NICOLAS LEDOUX (1736–1806); GEORGE DANCE (YOUNGER, 1741–1825); JOHN SOANE (1753–1837); CARLO ROSSI (1755–1849)

overpowering; expression; control; grandeur; reason; Enlightenment

The political philosopher Edmund Burke's famous contrast between the sublime and beautiful resonated throughout the arts in the late 18th century. Looking at ordered, regular objects induced a sense of repose and satisfaction he equated with beauty. By contrast, incomplete, jagged and restless views prompted feelings of awe and terror, even if they were not inherently frightening. This was the Sublime, and through garden design, the growing interest in ruins, and illustrations such as GB Piranesi's prison etchings, it found its way into architecture.

Claude-Nicolas Ledoux forged a highly personal Classical language out of inventive compositions that conjured Platonic solids into shapes adapted to, and expressive of their functions, with graphic detail to reinforce their symbolism. His tollgates, or *barrières*, built around Paris in the dying days of the *ancien régime,* brought awe to the expression of authority, and his unbuilt plans for an 'ideal city' refine the synthesis between elemental forms, function and symbolic detail.

Etienne-Louis Boullée's design for a Cenotaph for Newton (1784; unrealised) reflected the interest in science and reason, and the Neoclassical belief that pure solids – in this case the supremely impractical sphere – were the means to express them. But so vast is its scale that the enormity of the structure and the idea it represents are overwhelming, an impression made explicit in his equally unbuildable design for a monument dedicated to the Supreme Being.

On a smaller and more practical scale, John Soane, who met Piranesi and was later a friend of the painter JMW Turner, evoked the Sublime with shifting, restless spaces whose limits are hard to identify. Concealed light sources suggest unseen powers. Soane also used Gothic detail alongside Classicism, showing how conveying the Sublime not only revolutionised Classical architecture, but introduced the possibility of other traditions too.

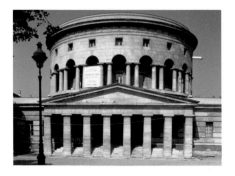

KEY BUILDINGS
← Barrière de la Villette, Paris, France, CLAUDE-NICOLAS LEDOUX, 1785–9
Just prior to the French Revolution of 1789, Ledoux designed a series of toll houses to collect royal taxes on goods brought into Paris. Despite their reactionary purpose, he experimented with revolutionary architectural ideas, at La Villette placing a cylinder on top of a Greek cross. Here, sparse ornament strengthens the pure volumes, as if generated by a raw force.

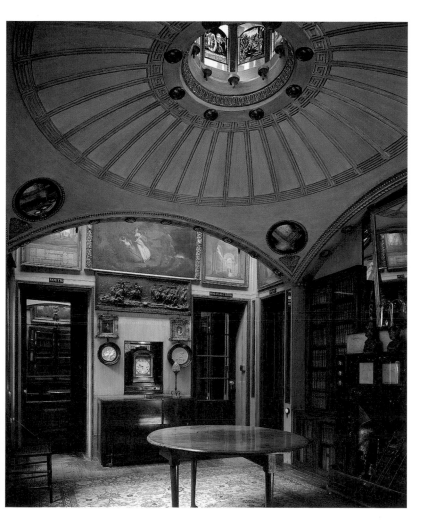

Breakfast Parlour, Sir John Soane's Museum, London, England, JOHN SOANE, 1812
Soane's design for this room in his own house suggests awe-inspiring phenomena beyond its immediately perceivable limits. A shallow dome defines the centre of the room, but light streams in from hidden windows above it, which when picked up by numerous mirrors suffuses the room in an ethereal glow. Carefully selected paintings add narrative associations to the overall effect.

OTHER BUILDINGS
All Hallows by the Tower, London, England, GEORGE DANCE (YOUNGER), 1765; Royal Saltworks, Arc-et-Senan, France, CLAUDE-NICOLAS LEDOUX, 1775–9; Bank of England, London, JOHN SOANE, from 1792; General Staff Headquarters, St Petersburg, Russia, CARLO ROSSI, 1819–29

 Baroque; Monumental Urbanism; Neoclassicism; Pre-Classicism; Imperialism

 Medievalism; Anti-Urbanism; Rococo

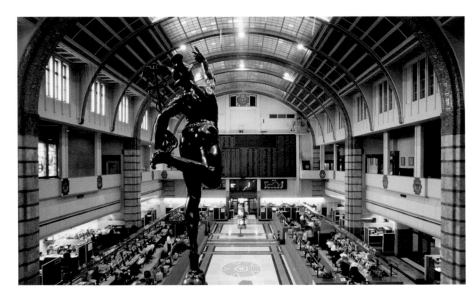

Once it became possible to calculate the lines of force within a structure, architectural theorists relished the chance to make a fetish out of practical mathematics. The intellectual contortions necessary to uphold this provide a seam of connective tissue between Neoclassicism, the Gothic Revival and Modernism.

JEAN NICOLAS LOUIS DURAND (1760–1834); HENRI LABROUSTE (1801–75); GOTTFRIED SEMPER (1803–79); AUGUSTUS PUGIN (1812–52); EUGÈNE VIOLLET-LE-DUC (1814–79); ANATOLE DE BAUDOT (1834–1915); HENDRICK BERLAGE (1856–1934); AUGUST PERRET (1874–1954)

Rationalism; logic; reason; order

The apparent rationality of science in determining where structural members should be placed fitted neatly with the Enlightenment striving for clarity. This helped shape Neoclassicism, but JNL Durand, who taught at the influential École Polytechnique in Paris from 1795, took the logic another step further in suggesting that architecture's intellectual base lay in science rather than in an unrecoverable mythical past. Its purpose was to translate the rationality of engineering into functional and logical plans with the aid of a regular square grid. Outwardly, this relegated decoration to a secondary role, but in severing the unity between structure and ornament it posed fundamental questions about the relationship between form, function and meaning.

Henri Labrouste's Bibliothèque Nationale suggested a new synthesis. Its plan is simple and rational and its structure is iron, but its decoration, though sparse and without departing entirely from Classical precedent, conveys a richly symbolic interpretation of its function as a library, and the relationship between language and architecture.

Both Eugène Viollet-le-Duc and Augustus Pugin used the rhetoric of Structural Rationalism to support their preference for Gothic. Pugin argued that Gothic's lack of any element that was not there for reasons of convenience, construction or propriety made it morally virtuous, while Viollet-le-Duc stressed Gothic's apparent derivation from structural principles.

By the early 20th century, architects like Hendrick Berlage began to explore the idea that structure itself could create space and allude to meaning without any need for decoration, a formula that reached its apogee in early Modernism.

KEY BUILDINGS
Stock Exchange, Amsterdam, the Netherlands, HENDRICK BERLAGE, 1897–1903
Berlage culled his concept of Structural Rationalism from eclectic sources, including Viollet-le-Duc and Semper. His intention was for the load-bearing brick structure not just to carry its weight in a logical manner, but to be inflected with corbels and other devices to demonstrate visually where the forces were going.

↓ Bibliothèque Nationale, Paris, France, HENRI LABROUSTE, 1860–8
Convinced that ornament should come from construction, Labrouste was one of the first architects to find expressive potential in iron. Its forms derived from the possibilities of the material, the Bibliothèque Nationale transcends stylistic precedents and anticipates later uses of metal in architecture.

OTHER BUILDINGS
FRANCE Bibliothèque Sainte Geneviève, Paris, HENRI LABROUSTE, 1845–50; St Denys-de-l'Estree, near Paris, VIOLLET-LE-DUC, 1864–7; St Jean de Montmartre, Paris, ANATOLE DE BAUDOT, 1897–1905; Notre Dame du Raincy, Paris, AUGUST PERRET, 1922–3

 Rationalism; Materialism

 Sublimism; Rococo; Expressionism

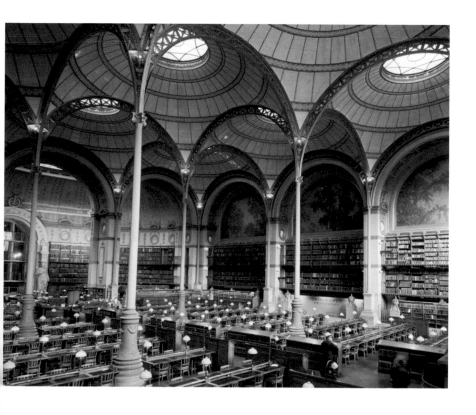

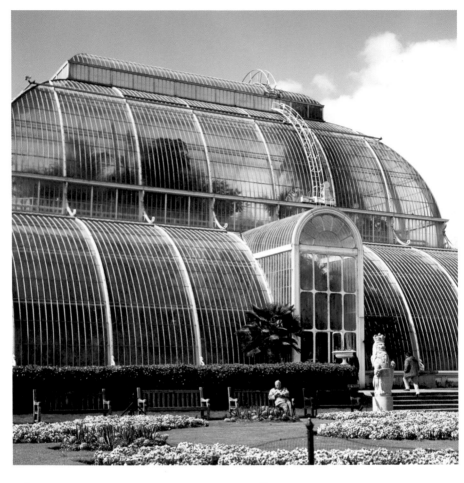

The question of whether iron and glass were appropriate materials for architecture vexed the architects of the mid-19th century, and because new building types such as railway stations had to use them, this was a question that could not be ignored. The central issue was whether the materials should be adapted to fit the canons of architecture that had evolved for millennia around stone and timber, or whether their constructional possibilities should be exploited without reference to tradition.

SYDNEY SMIRKE (1798–1877); LEWIS CUBITT (1799–1883); DECIMUS BURTON (1800–81); JOSEPH PAXTON (1801–65); PETER ELLIS (1804–84); ISAMBARD KINGDOM BRUNEL (1806–59); BENJAMIN WOODWARD (1816–61); MATTHEW DIGBY WYATT (1820–77)

material; iron; glass; decoration; structure

Iron's capability in providing effective structures, proved as early as 1779 in Abraham Darby's iron bridge at Coalbrookdale, set a time bomb under conventional architectural theory, predicated as it was on traditional materials and forms of construction. The fuse burnt slowly until the 1830s, when an increase in iron production and potential uses for it in new building types coincided with theorists such as Augustus Pugin who were arguing that architecture should be true to its materials. Numerous contortions followed. Romantic Medievalists wrote iron out of architecture altogether, others tried with varying degrees of success to find some balance between the constructional logic of iron and architectural conventions, while a small minority recognised its potential to create a new sort of architecture.

Despite the best efforts of collaborations such as that between Matthew Digby Wyatt and Isambard Kingdom Brunel to tame the raw engineering of Paddington Station with an architectural sensibility, Victorian thinker John Ruskin opined that though a genuinely architectural use of iron might eventually emerge, it had not by 1850. This inspired his disciple, Benjamin Woodward, to coerce the Coventry ironmaster Skidmore to contrive a 'Gothic' structure for the inner court of the Oxford Museum. But by then two seminal structures had already demonstrated the potential of iron to create entirely new types of enclosure: Joseph Paxton's vast Crystal Palace of 1851, built with extraordinary rapidity, great efficacy and evident prefabrication; and Decimus Burton and Richard Turner's magnificent Palm House at Kew, where the logic of iron fabrication and construction clearly overrides architectural convention.

St Pancras Station marked the point where any attempt at marrying iron construction and traditional styles was abandoned. This split between architecture and engineering echoed for several generations before reaching its climax in Modernism.

KEY BUILDINGS

← Palm House, Kew Gardens, London, England, DECIMUS BURTON and RICHARD TURNER (ironmaster), 1849
A palm house was an obvious project to demonstrate the potential of iron and glass to enclose a large volume in a relatively lightweight and transparent way. Turner's skill in iron-working complemented Burton's Neoclassical sensibilities to create a refined and highly original building in a new material, two years before the Crystal Palace.

↓ Natural History Museum, Oxford, England, THOMAS DEANE and BENJAMIN WOODWARD, 1854–8
Conceived by the university's leading scientist Thomas Acland as an index to natural history, and strongly influenced by his friend John Ruskin's concept of Gothic as the style closest to nature, the 'Gothicised' iron roof over the quadrangle shows the dichotomy between scientific progress and stylistic representation.

OTHER BUILDINGS
UK The Crystal Palace, London, JOSEPH PAXTON, 1851; Kings Cross Station, London, I FWIS CUBITT, 1850–2; Old Reading Room, British Museum, London, SYDNEY SMIRKE, 1852–7; Paddington Station, London, ISAMBARD KINGDOM BRUNEL and MATTHEW DIGBY WYATT, 1854; Oriel Chambers, Liverpool, PETER ELLIS, 1864–5

 Structural Rationalism; Industrialism

Expressionism; Baroque

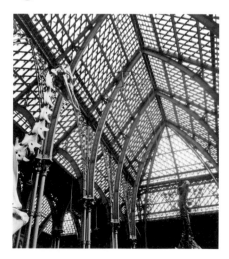

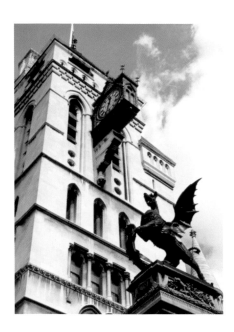

Medievalists believed Medieval society displayed moral virtues that either Enlightenment thinking or industrialisation had destroyed. Even if it was impossible to recreate that society, replicating its artefacts would have the instructive benefit of spreading those virtues among those who actually made them, and those who used and saw them. Aesthetics took a specifically moral and didactic twist.

AUGUSTUS PUGIN (1812–52); WILLIAM BUTTERFIELD (1814–1900); EUGÈNE VIOLLET-LE-DUC (1814–79); JOHN LOUGHBOROUGH PEARSON (1817–97); GEORGE EDMUND STREET (1824–81); WILLIAM BURGES (1827–81)

medieval; Gothic; ornament; detail

Social and religious crises in the 1830s and 1840s brought a new intensity to the Gothic Revival, turning it from a plaything for wealthy dilettantes into an earnest exponent of social engineering. Augustus Pugin, a fervent Roman Catholic convert and prolific architect, argued that the key to dealing with the social ills provoked by industrialisation was to recreate the society of the late Middle Ages by imitating its architecture. Being both logical and moral, it should be copied exactly, not with the louche laxity of the 'Gothick'.

In France, Eugène Viollet-le-Duc developed Pugin's claims for Gothic's logic into a fully fledged Structural Rationalism. The moral line was most eloquently expanded by the Victorian thinker John Ruskin, who claimed that Gothic's 'changefulness' made it an extension of nature and, therefore, God's work. Its moral reach spread from the use of buildings to their construction, as the 'freedom' of self-expression it gave workers released them from the 'slavery' that Ruskin believed copying Classical detail to be. Somewhere between Pugin's Catholicism and Ruskin's Evangelical Christianity, the High Anglican Ecclesiological Society prescribed modifications to old churches and strictures for new designs.

Under these combined influences, most public buildings in Britain, from the Houses of Parliament (1835–60) to the Royal Courts of Justice (1868–82) took on some form of Gothic. Even when the limitations of historical revivalism became apparent, the influence of Pugin and Ruskin resurfaced in the Arts and Crafts movement, which adopted Pugin's cry for 'honest' construction and Ruskin's interest in the freedom of expression for workers.

KEY BUILDINGS
↑ All Saints, Margaret Street, London, England, WILLIAM BUTTERFIELD, 1850–59
This was the showcase for the Ecclesiological Society, a body of clergymen and architects who believed spiritual renewal could be achieved through correct application

of revived architecture, fittings and liturgy. Though subscribing to their beliefs, Butterfield was original in his proportions and composition to fit on to the tight urban site, and extraordinarily inventive in decoration.

Royal Courts of Justice, London, England, GEORGE EDMUND STREET, 1868–82

In the most important Gothic Revival building in London after the Houses of Parliament, Street achieved a much more scholarly and convincing recreation of the 13th-century Gothic that was thought to have suitably didactic and associative qualities for an institution that was meant to symbolise contemporary Britain and improve the execution of justice.

OTHER BUILDINGS

UK Cardiff Castle, Wales, WILLIAM BURGES, 1868–85; St Augustine's, Ramsgate, AUGUSTUS PUGIN, 1846–51; St James the Less, London, GEORGE EDMUND STREET, 1858–61; St Augustine's Kilburn, London, JOHN LOUGHBOROUGH PEARSON, 1870–80

Gothic Commercialism; Gothic Scholasticism; Victorianism; Anti-Urbanism

Neoclassicism; Decorative Industrialism; Monumental Urbanism

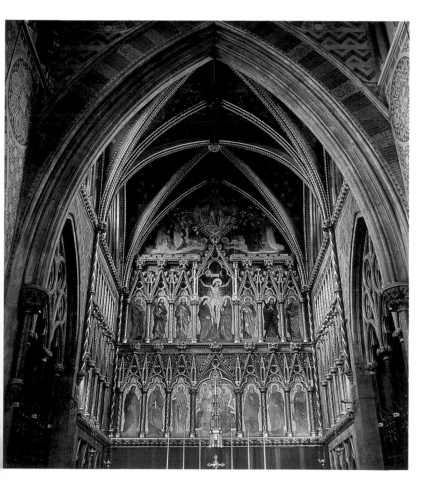

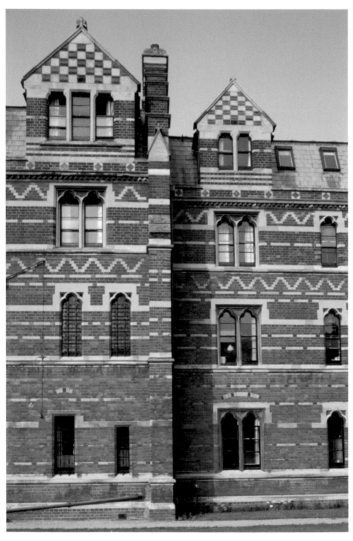

Victorian architecture is often characterised as a battle of the styles, between Gothic and Classical. However, the struggle actually lay deeper than this, in a profound desire to bring an understanding of new technologies and social change, incorporating them within architectural tradition.

CHARLES BARRY (1795–1860); ANTHONY SALVIN (1799–1881); GEORGE GILBERT SCOTT (1811–77); AUGUSTUS PUGIN (1812–52); WILLIAM BUTTERFIELD (1814–1900); ALFRED WATERHOUSE (1830–1905)

monumentality; didacticism; Urbanism; industrialism

Victorian architecture is representative of a society caught between extraordinary technological progress and deference to the authority of tradition. This tension generated elephantine buildings that were decorated with details derived from historical architecture, but on a scale and using techniques that were unthinkable before the 19th century. Historical styles could still communicate the values they represented, even though little more than a dressing for entirely new functions, or transformed out of all recognition by the enormous social changes underway. Industrially produced historical ornaments questioned whether ornament had to be made in the same way as it had been traditionally in order to convey the same meaning?

New means of financing, and the organisation of labour permitted massive engineering works like railways and drainage systems, making possible conurbations of ever-increasing size. New building types, such as stations, could only be constructed using new technologies and materials like iron and glass. As such types had no precedent in the Classical or Gothic worlds, their architectural treatment was problematic. Responses ranged from the unadorned structure of the St Pancras train shed, to the gargantuan Gothic of the Midland Hotel in front of it, which uses iron and plate glass equally lavishly.

Even a building type as traditional as an Oxford college betrays the temperament of the time. Keble College broke with precedent. It was cheaper and less grand than its august precedents, in part because Butterfield, unlike many of his peers, was prepared to use industrially produced materials and new ways of organising the construction process. A large donation from the Gibbs family helped too.

KEY BUILDINGS

← Keble College, Oxford University, England, WILLIAM BUTTERFIELD, 1868–82
Butterfield sought to create a version of the Gothic that took advantage of 19th-century technological and social changes. He used mass-produced bricks and tiles, and by taking responsibility for the design of ornamentation himself, rather than delegating it to individual workers, he approached what became the standard relationship between architect and builder.

→ St Pancras Station, London, England, GEORGE GILBERT SCOTT (Midland Hotel), 1868–74, and WILLIAM HENRY BARLOW (train shed), 1863–5
St Pancras captures the Victorian dilemma. Even where Gothic could be stretched to an unprecedented size for the hotel, offices and booking hall, it could not meet the functional requirements for the train shed (just visible to the right), which had to rise to a certain height so the steam could escape. No attempt was made to integrate the two parts architecturally; they merely adjoin.

OTHER BUILDINGS
UK Harlaxton Manor, Lincolnshire, ANTHONY SALVIN, 1834–55; Houses of Parliament, London, CHARLES BARRY and AUGUSTUS PUGIN, 1835–68; Foreign Office, London, GEORGE GILBERT SCOTT, 1860–75

 Medievalism; Monumental Urbanism; Decorative Industrialism

 Neoclassicism; Anti-Urbanism

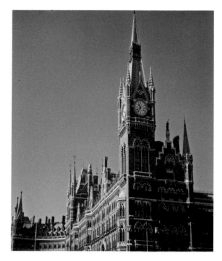

The massive expansion of cities in the 19th century meant that changed construction methods and developments in economic and social activity spawned new building types, while social and political upheaval provoked demand for new institutions, streets and vistas. Concepts of cities as they had evolved from the Renaissance could not meet these challenges, thus architects and urban planners felt their way towards new patterns of Urbanism.

JEAN-FRANÇOIS THÉRÈSE CHALGRIN (1739–1811); **CHARLES BARRY** (1795–1860); **GOTTFRIED SEMPER** (1803–79); **JOSEPH POELART** (1817–79); **CHARLES GARNIER** (1825–98); **DANIEL BURNHAM** (1846–1912)

grandeur; commemoration; power; bombast; imposition

In the 1830s and 1840s, urban institutions became more numerous and served increasingly complex functions. In his London clubs and, above all, the Houses of Parliament, Charles Barry consummately adapted historic models to modern needs. Outwardly, Gottfried Semper's Dresden Opera House also borrows historical forms. But, by resolving the complex volumetric requirements for his friend Richard Wagner's operatic innovations into an accomplished urban monument, he used contemporary needs to create a new monumental form. His writings sought a synthesis between expanding archaeological discoveries and new technology that went beyond existing stylistic classifications.

By the mid-19th century, city-wide solutions became necessary. London, Vienna and Paris made three archetypal responses. London's was practical, creating the Metropolitan Board of Works to solve public health problems, but massive engineering works soon affected all parts of the city.

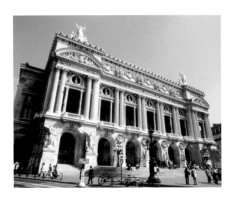

More overtly aesthetic, Vienna converted its fortifications into the Ringstrasse, where bourgeois institutions asserted themselves in monumental buildings with styles chosen for their symbolic relation to function, such as in the Neo-Greek parliament. Their isolation was later criticised by Camillo Sitte, who argued for a close integration between activities and forms within and outside public buildings.

In 1850, Georges-Eugène Haussmann became prefect of Paris. Turning the city into a giant workshop and showcase, he cut straight streets through its historic fabric, lined them with standard buildings and marked their junctions with monuments, such as Charles Garnier's Opera. In wrapping social, technical and economic issues into an aesthetic, this became a standard model. Daniel Burnham adapted it to beautify Chicago, the iconic city of American industrial expansion, overlaying a system of vistas radiating out from civic monuments over the original urban grid in his unrealised plan of 1909.

KEY BUILDINGS

Opera Garnier, Paris, France, CHARLES GARNIER,
1861–74
Most spectacular of the great public institutions in
Austrian engineer Baron George Eugene Haussmann's
transformation of Paris, the opera is deliberately
positioned at the junction of several long, straight
boulevards. Its opulent facade reinforces the
overwhelming effect by combining Neoclassical
motifs with busts of great composers to make a visual
connection between function and architectural tradition.

Kunsthistorisches Museum, Vienna, Austria,
GOTTFRIED SEMPER, 1869
The museum forms one side of Semper's monumental
conception for the Outer Burgplatz, part of the
Ringstrasse development that transformed Vienna's old
fortifications into a series of urban landmarks. With the
Natural History Museum, it flanks the Hofburg (Imperial
Palace), symbolically uniting emperor and bourgeois
culture in a manner and on a scale impossible before
the 19th century.

OTHER BUILDINGS

L'Arc de Triomphe, Paris, France, JEAN-FRANÇOIS
THÉRÈSE CHALGRIN, 1806–35; Marble Arch, London,
England, JOHN NASH, 1828; Trafalgar Square, London,
CHARLES BARRY, 1840; Palais de Justice, Brussels,
Belgium, JOSEPH POELART, 1866–83; Vittorio
Emmanuele II monument, Rome, Italy, GIUSEPPE
SACCONI, 1885–1911; World's Fair Site, Chicago,
Illinois, US, DANIEL BURNHAM, 1893

 Roman Classicism; Baroque; Pre-Classicism

Ecoism; Humanism; Rationalism

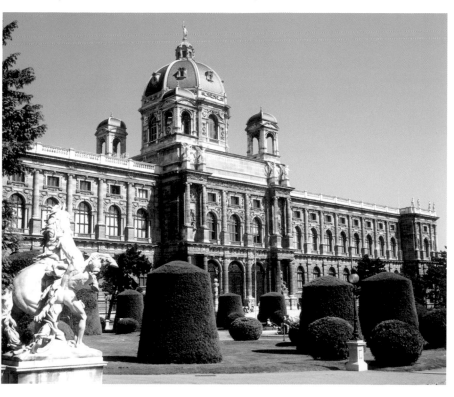

Country living seemed an attractive alternative to the squalor of industrial cities, but it proved extremely difficult to disentangle genuine concerns for social improvement from nostalgia for the social relations of a pre-industrial society. Architecture at the end of the 19th century reflected this dilemma between progressive ideals and traditional appearances.

PHILIP WEBB (1831–1915); **NORMAN SHAW** (1831–1912); **CHARLES FRANCIS ANNESLEY VOYSEY** (1857–1941); **RAYMOND UNWIN** (1863–1940); **MACKAY HUGH BAILLIE SCOTT** (1865–1945); **BARRY PARKER** (1867–1941); **FRANK LLOYD WRIGHT** (1867–1959)

garden city; suburb; rural idyll; the great wen; simplicity; homespun; temperance; social relations; community; communal ownership

Although the decorative and plagiaristic aspects of the Gothic Revival had burnt themselves out by the 1880s, its legacy of romanticised nostalgia and puritanism survived to shape the Arts and Crafts and Garden City movements. British craftsman, designer, writer and Socialist William Morris preached the virtues of a simple, rural and quasi-medieval life, which Philip Webb – who designed the Red House for Morris – attempted and, occasionally, almost succeeded in embodying in his buildings.

The Arts and Crafts movement vested architecture's power to express ideas in traditional building crafts, severing any connection with contemporary concerns such as industrialisation and urban expansion, and ultimately limiting the scope of what architecture could convey. In individual buildings, compositional geniuses like Norman Shaw, Charles Voysey and MH Baillie Scott could transcend the incipient nostalgia, but never overcame the underlying contradiction of using traditional means to solve problems of modern life.

It was left to the parliamentary stenographer Ebenezer Howard to propose a comprehensive strategy for new patterns of Urbanism in his *Tomorrow: A Peaceful Path to Real Reform* (1898). Co-operative ownership, Howard argued, would allow a more equitable use of land where settlements could be controlled in size and density so that everyone was near a centre of employment, but also had access to open land. Though he prescribed no obvious architectural idiom, his Anti-Urban sentiments chimed with Arts and Crafts aims. When Raymond Unwin and Barry Parker were appointed to design the first garden city, Letchworth (1903),

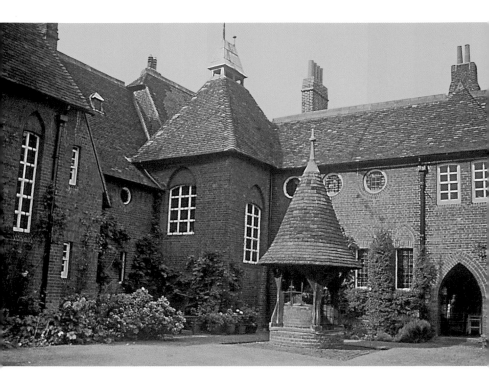

they ensured that vernacular architectural features would infuse the lexicon of garden-city life as much as the craft and co-operative values.

Garden-city ideals spread across the world in many different forms. One version underpinned Imperial capitals like Canberra and New Delhi; another fed into communal experiments in the Soviet Union.

↑ The Red House, Bexleyheath, England, PHILIP WEBB, 1859
The enormous praise heaped on Webb's design belied the enervating nervousness of its affected simplicity. Built for the independently wealth William Morris, who urged social revolution via a regression to the Middle Ages, the Red House introduced the idea of a simplified, rural idyll.

OTHER BUILDINGS
UK Bedford Park, London, NORMAN SHAW, 1876; Letchworth Garden City, RAYMOND UNWIN and BARRY PARKER, from 1903; Hampstead Garden Suburb, London, RAYMOND UNWIN, with work by EDWIN LUTYENS and HM BAILLIE SCOTT, from 1906

US Robie House, Chicago, FRANK LLOYD WRIGHT, 1909 (plus numerous houses in Oak Park, Illinois)

KEY BUILDINGS
Waldbuhl House, Uzwil, Switzerland, **MH BAILLIE SCOTT, 1907–11**
Baillie Scott was one of the most inventive architects of the English Arts and Crafts movement, and managed to combine clear and workable plans with convincing recreations or adaptations of traditional detail. Even when working in Switzerland, he adapted traditional English features, such as half-timbering.

Exoticism; Functionalism

Decorative Industrialism; Rococo; Rationalism

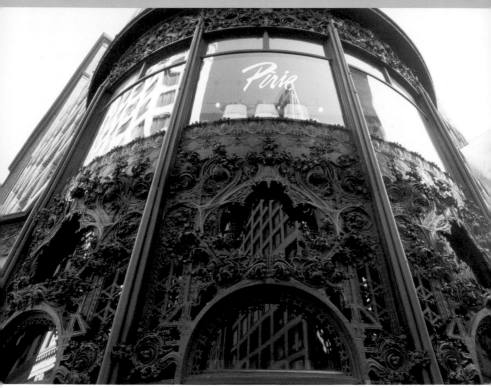

From the late 19th century, architects began to realise that industrially produced materials could not just create unprecedented forms and structures, but could be developed into new decorative languages as well. Buoyed by new aesthetic theories, this potential to infuse 'spirit', or artistic content into the inanimate and otherwise impersonal products of industrialism opened the door to new syntheses between physical objects and ideas.

OTTO WAGNER (1841–1918); ANTONIO GAUDÍ (1852–1926); LOUIS SULLIVAN (1856–1924); WILLIAM LETHABY (1857–1931); VICTOR HORTA (1861–1947); HENRI VAN DE VELDE (1863–1957); JOSEF MARIA OLBRICH (1867–1908); HECTOR GUIMARD (1867–1942); PETER BEHRENS (1868–1940); JOSEF HOFFMANN (1870–1956)

expression; sinuous line; decoration; emblem; fluidity

As industrialisation was changing society beyond recognition, intellectuals questioned whether it also changed notions of beauty. These questions were most intense where the effects of industrialisation were strongest, such as in Chicago and Berlin. August Endell argued that the beauty of such cities could not be judged by conventional standards. But architects in Vienna, Paris, Brussels, Barcelona and the Nordic countries all looked outside the Classical tradition, to sources as varied as technology and national myths, to find new means of expression.

The urge to unite art and industry became almost universal, from William Lethaby in

Decorative Industrialism

the UK to Henri van de Velde in the Weimar School of Applied Arts, which later became the Bauhaus. Peter Behrens, as designer for AEG, came closest to achieving it in his designs for household goods, though apart from his turbine factory his architecture was less successful.

But each location had specific variations. In Paris and Brussels, Hector Guimard and Victor Horta incorporated flowing, tendril-like lines that departed from the rigidities of Beaux-Arts Classicism. Furthermore, ornaments such as Guimard's Metro entrances could only be made in iron. Antonio Gaudí demonstrated his belief that the curved line belonged to God in his extraordinary Sagrada Família Church, where curves are not just decoration, but an inherent part of the structure. And in Vienna, Otto Wagner argued that Modern architecture was an iteration between tradition and modernity. His masterpiece, the Post Office Savings Bank, exploited the decorative potential of aluminium, then in its infancy.

The steel frame totally transformed buildings in Chicago. Louis Sullivan accepted its proportional discipline and devised inventive ornamentation based on natural forms, bypassing Classicism's relationship between regular structure and stylised decoration.

KEY BUILDINGS

← Carson Pirie Scott department store, Chicago, Illinois, US, LOUIS SULLIVAN, 1899
Department stores were a new building type made possible by the steel frame. Sullivan's design combines the two in a new architectural order. He conceived the decorative metalwork on the ground and first floors as if they were picture frames for the window displays, while the plain floors above express the proportions of the steel.

↓ Metro entrance, Porte Dauphine, Paris, France, HECTOR GUIMARD, 1900
Guimard's metro entrances, designed between 1899 and 1904, are not just the epitome of Paris's Belle Epoque, with their exuberant, flowing forms in wrought iron. They also use new technology to decorate and celebrate the new infrastructure of the Metro, which itself made an enormous contribution to the city's status as a modern metropolis.

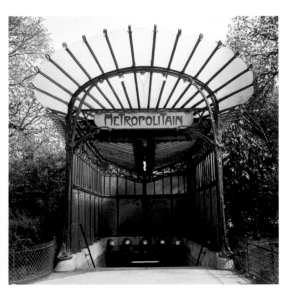

OTHER BUILDINGS
Sagrada Família Church, Barcelona, Spain, ANTONIO GAUDÍ, from 1883; Castel Berenger, Paris, France, HECTOR GUIMARD, 1894–8; Maison du Peuple, Brussels, Belgium, VICTOR HORTA, 1896–7; Secession Building, Vienna, Austria, JOSEF MARIA OLBRICH, 1898; Post Office Savings Bank, Vienna, OTTO WAGNER, 1904–06; Palais Stoclet, Brussels, JOSEF HOFFMANN, 1905–11

 Neoclassicism; Rationalism; Neo-Rationalism

 Baroque; Expressionism; Postmodernism

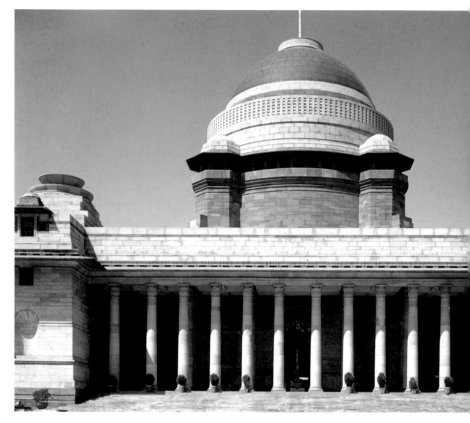

Colonialism brought European and non-European cultures into contact with one another, causing sporadic effects on their various architectural traditions. Imperialism describes the architecture in the colonies themselves, where such contact was most intense and reflected the complicated interaction between rulers and ruled. As the aesthetic syntheses became more sophisticated, architecture increasingly became an explicit tool of Imperial policy.

CHARLES MANT (1839–81); **ROBERT CHISHOLM** (1840–1915); **SWINTON JACOB** (1841–1917); **WILLIAM EMERSON** (1843–1921); **HERBERT BAKER** (1862–1946); **EDWIN LUTYENS** (1869–1944)

orientalism; administration; colonialism; representation

The earliest colonial buildings reflected European models, but local climates, materials and building techniques soon led to a variety of modifications. In India, which had the richest architectural tradition of the colonised territories, most colonial buildings were designed by military engineers, and through these imperfect models Neoclassicism joined the numerous waves of foreign architectural imports. Indian princes slowly began to incorporate European elements into their palaces, and British interest turned towards

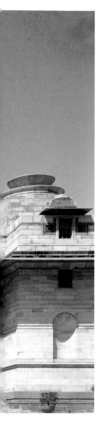

understanding indigenous architecture. Its bewildering complexity seemed to reflect India's political diversity. However, engineers and, later, architects in the public works department began to devise a composite style called Indo-Saracenic.

Drawing, at least superficially, on various traditions, this style codified the two British assumptions that Hindu and Saracenic architecture were unrelated, and that only in their hands could the two cultures be peacefully united. Its political implications were made explicit in monuments such as Charles Mant's Mayo College, where Indian princes were educated, and numerous memorials to viceroys and Queen Victoria.

New Delhi, conceived in 1910, continued and ended this policy. Its principal architect, Edwin Lutyens, expressed contempt for Indian architecture, but nevertheless incorporated various pared-down elements from it in his masterpiece, the Viceroy's House. Less consummate, but even more convinced of his legitimacy, was Herbert Baker, who made his reputation splicing the modest Cape Dutch style to the Arts and Crafts idiom for super-rich 'Randlords' in South Africa. His collaboration with Lutyens in Delhi ended in acrimony, but his Union

Buildings in Pretoria, started in 1909 to symbolise the 'union' of South Africa after the Anglo-Boer War, was similarly grandiose. Nelson Mandela's selection of it for his presidential inauguration in 1994 shows how the impact of such a building can outlive its original purpose.

KEY BUILDINGS

← Viceroy's House, New Delhi, India, EDWIN LUTYENS, 1912–30
Lutyens put into practice his mastery of complex geometry in this centrepiece of the new capital of India, incorporating a limited symbolic union between Indian and European architecture, but also creating a composition that rises above and dominates its setting on a plain littered with ruins of earlier cities.

→ Union Buildings, Pretoria, South Africa, HERBERT BAKER, 1909–12
Baker envisaged an Imperial acropolis for the capital of the Union of South Africa, created in 1910 from two British colonies and two independent Boer republics. Two main buildings atop a hill overlooking the city are symbolically joined by a curving colonnade.

OTHER BUILDINGS
INDIA Madras University Senate House, ROBERT CHISHOLM, 1874–9; Mayo College, Rajasthan, CHARLES MANT, 1875–9; Laxmi Vilas Palace, Baroda, SWINTON JACOB, 1881–90; Victoria Memorial, Calcutta, WILLIAM EMERSON, 1901–21; Secretariat Buildings, New Delhi, HERBERT BAKER, 1912–30; India Arch, New Delhi, EDWIN LUTYENS, 1921–31

Monumental Urbanism; Pre-Classicism; Indism; Exoticism

Regionalism; Medievalism

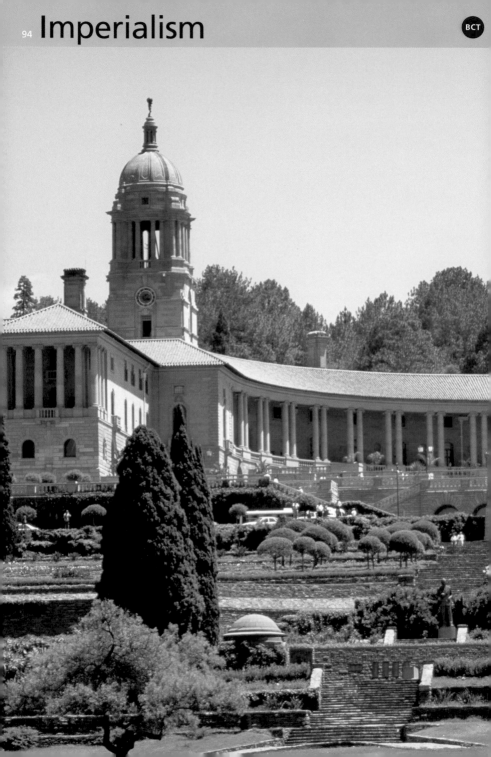

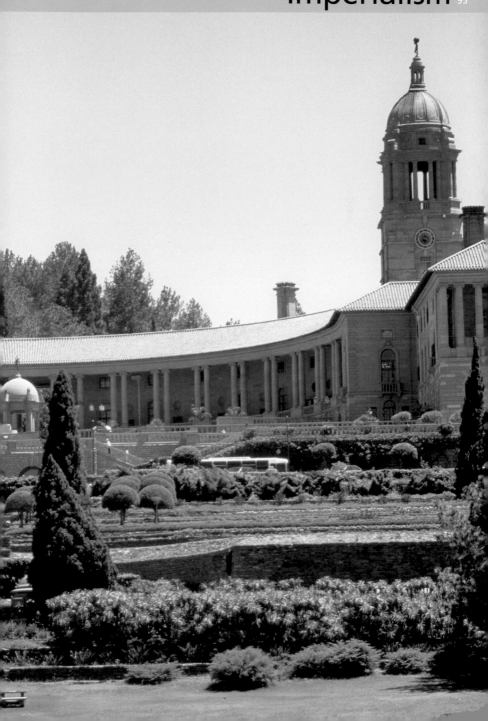

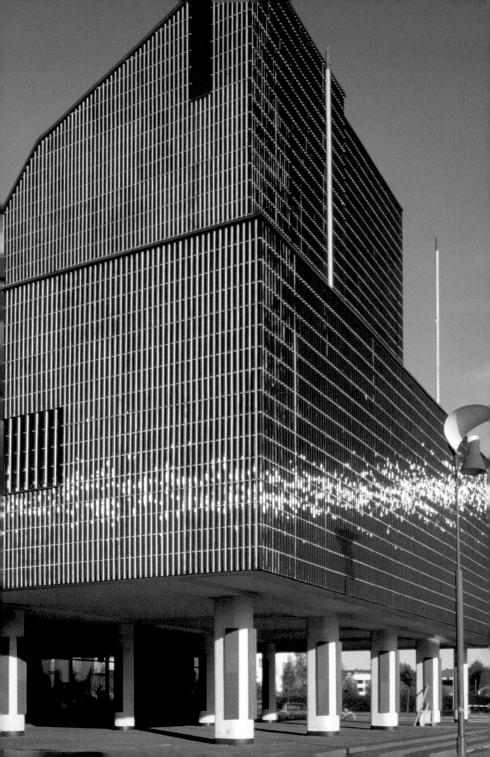

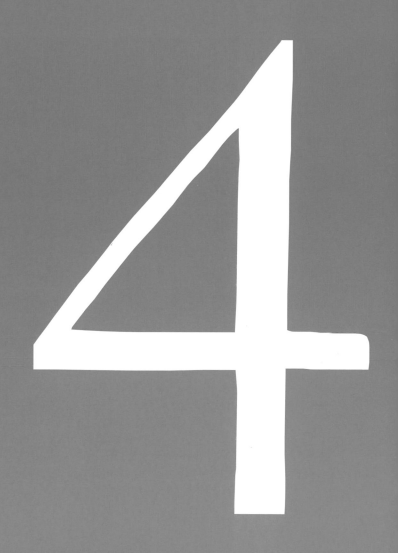

MODERNISM

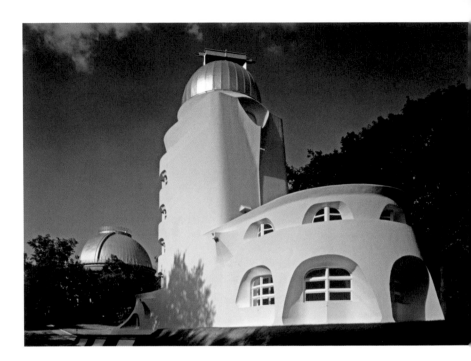

More a state of mind than a defined movement, Expressionism arose from the assumption that a building could convey an individual idea or thought without mediation by architectural conventions or styles. Its potential for dramatic gestures became apparent immediately after the First World War, when it provided a rallying point for what became Modern architecture.

PETER BEHRENS (1868–1940);
HANS POELZIG (1869–1936); FRITZ HÖGER (1877–1949); BRUNO TAUT (1880–1938);
MICHEL DE KLERK (1884–1923); PIETER KRAMER (1881–1961); ERICH MENDELSOHN (1887–1953);
GIOVANNI MICHELUCCI (1891–1990);
EERO SAARINEN (1910–61); JØRN UTZON (1918–);
GÜNTER BEHNISCH (1922–)

expression; restlessness; instability; anthropomorphism

Industrial buildings, with their requirement for bold volumes and lack of precedents, first provided architects with a licence to experiment with dramatic forms in the years up to 1914. An early example was Hans Poelzig's extraordinary combination of water tower and exhibition hall in Poznan, Poland, in 1911. However, from 1918 onwards numerous architects, mainly in Germany, experimented with irregular shapes and dramatic effects. These were often deliberately unbuildable gestures, such as Mies van der Rohe's glass skyscrapers, but no less potent as polemics. A more practical counterpart was the work of the Amsterdam School, notably in housing, whose almost anthropomorphic forms enlivened the city's southern extension in the 1920s.

Both Constructivism and Functionalism share the powerful and sometimes outlandish shapes of Expressionism, but with important differences. Constructivism was an attempt to devise a new aesthetic based on machines and, ultimately, science, and Functionalism tried to derive forms from the activities or functions they accommodated. At its purest, Expressionism sought no justification beyond the existence of an idea in the mind of the architect.

Erich Mendelsohn's Einstein Tower in Potsdam (1917–21) brought Expressionism to its apogee in its attempt to translate the famous physicist's formulae into flowing architectural forms, as if forging a new relationship between space and time. Like Mendelsohn, most practitioners of Expressionism later settled down – often moving into Functionalism or Rationalism. However, Expressionism did provide a vital outlet for experimenting in formal ideas at a time when all authority and precedent seemed questionable.

Expressionist forms continued to interest architects, especially those on the geographic fringes of Modernism, such as the Danish architect Jørn Utzon, whose Sydney Opera House sublimates function and context to an extraordinarily powerful series of forms.

KEY BUILDINGS

← Einstein Tower, Potsdam, Germany, ERICH MENDELSOHN, 1917–21
As an observatory and astrophysics laboratory, the name had obvious significance and, together with its streamlined sculptural form, the design is the epitome of the search for a relationship between new functions and new forms that marked the period around 1920.

↓ Sydney Opera House, Sydney, Australia, JØRN UTZON, 1956–73
Utzon was one of the first architects to exploit the expressive potential of concrete shell structures (and the engineering skills of Ove Arup and Partners) in devising a memorable form, injecting life into a staid city.

OTHER BUILDINGS
GERMANY Glashaus at the Werkbund-Austellung (exhibition), Cologne, BRUNO TAUT, 1914; Hoechst Dyeworks, Frankfurt, PETER BEHRENS, 1920–5; Chilehaus, Hamburg, FRITZ HÖGER, 1922–3; Olympiapark, Munich, GÜNTER BEHNISCH, 1967–72

THE NETHERLANDS Eigen Haard housing, Amsterdam, MICHEL DE KLERK, 1921

US TWA Terminal, JFK Airport, New York, EERO SAARINEN, 1958–62

ITALY San Giovanni Battista, Florence, GIOVANNI MICHELUCCI, 1960–3

 Medievalism; Decorative Industrialism; Constructivism; Deconstructivism

 Rationalism; Corporatism; Neoclassicism; Neo-Rationalism

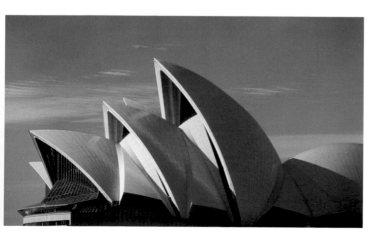

Frank Lloyd Wright coined the term
Usonian from the US to describe what
he considered to be the authentically
American values of his relatively low-cost
houses of the 1930s. For much of his long
career he was the pre-eminent architect in
the US, and at the forefront of its attempts
to find an architecture that expressed
national and contemporary ideas.

LOUIS SULLIVAN (1856–1924); **BERNARD
MAYBECK** (1862–1957); **FRANK LLOYD
WRIGHT** (1867–1959); **CHARLES & HENRY GREENE**
(1868–1957, 1870–1954); **ALBERT KAHN** (1869–
1942); **GEORGE HOWE** (1886–1955); **RUDOLPH
SCHINDLER** (1887–1953); **RICHARD NEUTRA**
(1892–1970); **WILLIAM LESCAZE** (1896–1969);
LOUIS KAHN (1901–74); **BRUCE GOFF** (1904–82)

freedom; democracy;
national identity

By the 1890s, American architecture
was striking out on several distinct
paths. The East Coast shingle style and Bay
style in California both combined complex
compositions and eclectic detailing with
innovative interior planning. However, in
Chicago, architects began to forge an
entirely new architecture from the steel frame,
the elevator, and industrially produced
details and ornaments. Louis Sullivan, one of
its leading architects, believed that in
architecture, as in nature, form derived from
the essence of the task it served.

Wright went further than his *Lieber
meister* in seeking a unity between form and
function which, reflecting his love of nature,
he called 'organic architecture'. His early
prairie houses appear tied to the ground

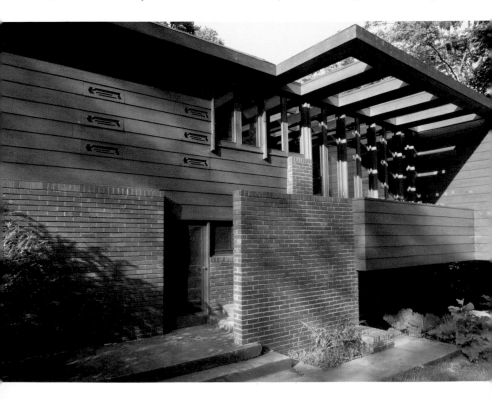

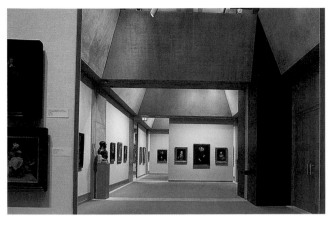

KEY BUILDINGS

← Yale University Art Gallery, New Haven, Connecticut, US, LOUIS KAHN, 1951–4
Kahn's first major commission was an eloquent critique of the increasingly banal Modernism imported to the US from Europe. In the Yale gallery, he introduced sculptural effects in the roof structure and central staircase to articulate an otherwise free plan, transforming American architecture rather as abstract Expressionism was transforming painting.

with their strong horizontal lines, while their innovative planning introduces new concepts of space and composition. The Usonian houses of the 1930s attempted to bring such an architecture within reach of all, or at least more Americans. Even more spatially complex, but simpler in construction to reduce cost, they were equally tied to their sites and the lifestyles of their clients.

Wright's former employees Rudolf Schindler and Richard Neutra developed some of these principles when they moved to California, but Wright was generally dismissive of other architects, and particularly contemptuous of European Modernists. Also ambiguous is his relationship to another great American architect, Louis Kahn, who also explored interactions between form, function and structure. Though he showed some affinity for the social ideals of European Modernists, from the 1950s onwards Kahn produced a stream of formally and compositionally inventive designs. His influence as an architect and teacher was extensive and somewhat surprising: his students included the greatest American Postmodernists Charles Moore and Robert Venturi.

≪ Greg Affleck House, Bloomfield Hills, Michigan, US, FRANK LLOYD WRIGHT, 1941
Associated throughout his long career with the search for an authentically American architecture, during the 1930s Wright investigated simple and standardised construction methods to bring his architecture to a wider public. The Greg Affleck House is one of the resulting Usonian houses which, with subtle planning, manages to create inventive effects with space, light and texture.

OTHER BUILDINGS
US Gamble House, Pasadena, California, GREENE AND GREENE, 1908–9; Lovell Beach House, Newport Beach, California, RUDOLPH SCHINDLER, 1925–6; Lovell House, Los Angeles, California, RICHARD NEUTRA, 1927–9; PSFS Skyscraper, Philadelphia, Pennsylvania, GEORGE HOWE AND LESCAZE, 1929–32; Bavinger House, Norman, Oklahoma, BRUCE GOFF, 1950–05

 Regionalism; Anti-Urbanism; Postmodernism

 Rationalism; Purism

Constructivism

Constructivism is the most enduringly influential of the radical architectural movements that flourished briefly in the Soviet Union between the October Revolution of 1917 and the imposition of Socialist Realism at the end of the 1920s. Although largely abstract and consciously non-referential, some examples reflect the powerful forms of heavy engineering, perhaps suggesting that naked, yet romanticised, science might replace traditional Russian values as the spiritual content of art.

KONSTANTIN MELNIKOV (1890–1974); VLADIMIR TATLIN (1885–1953); LEONID, VIKTOR & ALEXANDER VESNIN (1880–1933, 1882–1950, 1883–1959); IVAN LEONIDOV (1902–59); NIKOLAI MILIUTIN (1889–1942)

Radicalism; social condenser; experiment; avant-garde; art and society; renewal; agitprop

Constructivism emerged from two assumptions: that architecture could reflect and even help to call the new Soviet society into being, and that biology and physics would provide a rational basis for it. There was consequently no need for artistic tradition, and by engaging with social progress, architecture would serve supposedly real needs. Scientific processes would generate new forms with no reference to tradition.

Initially, Constructivism found an outlet in temporary polemical artworks, but its scope was wide. Miliutin proposed an ideal form for a Socialist town, while others turned their attention to 'social condensers', new buildings and institutions that would help bring about the new society. Notable are the powerful, angular forms of Melnikov's workers' clubs in Moscow, which draw on the large-scale industrial structures the Soviet Union was so keen to promote, and which monumentalised working-class organisations.

Vladimir Tatlin's Monument to the Third International, though it never went beyond the planning stages, underpins Constructivism's dilemmas. Its purpose is authentically Socialist, and its form follows a logarithmic sequence, yet it also clearly refers to the Eiffel Tower.

In its fascination with developing engineering products into an abstract formal language, Constructivism belongs among the experimental movements of the early 1920s that form the components of Modernism. It is also indelibly Russian, springing from the fierce post-Revolution polemics about how art could express aspects of everyday life. Subjectivity inevitably intervened in determining how even supposedly objective science might be translated into built form. So Constructivism existed on the dangerous edge between functional design and subjective art, making it an easy target once subjectivity became politically suspect to the Soviet regime. Nevertheless, in samizdat form it survived to inspire architects outside the Soviet Union for several generations.

KEY BUILDING
→ Monument to the Third International, VLADIMIR TATLIN, 1920
Tatlin's famous tower, here shown in reconstruction, captures both the structural dynamism and temporary, almost fairground-like nature of early Constructivist designs. Science and agitprop street art would combine to lead the people towards a new non-bourgeois culture.

OTHER BUILDINGS
RUSSIA Design for Pravda Building, Moscow, ALEXANDER VESNIN, 1923; Lenin Institute, Moscow, IVAN LEONIDOV, 1927; Rusakov Club, Moscow, KONSTANTIN MELNIKOV, 1927–8

UKRAINE Dneprostroi Dam, VIKTOR VESNIN, 1932

Expressionism; Deconstructivism; Functionalism

Rationalism; Postmodernism

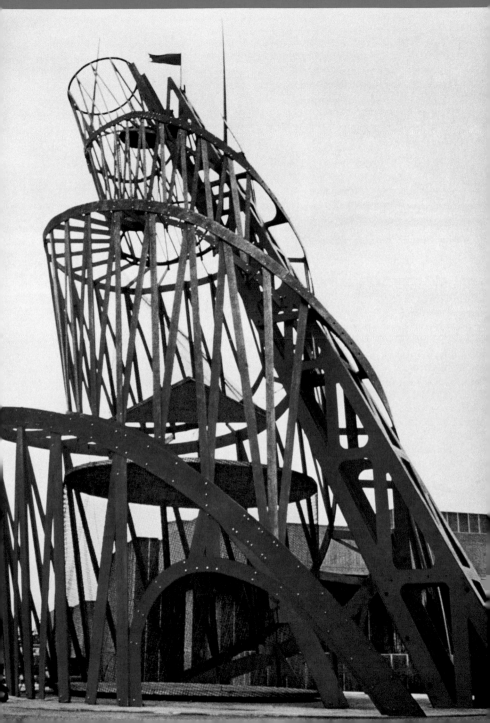

Architects responded immediately to the revolutions in visual culture that took place in Paris from Impressionism onwards, though the initial results were often eclectic and confused, and their influence from given 'isms' hard to trace precisely. But in the post-Cubist 1920s, largely through Le Corbusier, Modern art and architecture developed aesthetics that clearly shared common elements.

LE CORBUSIER (1887–1965); ANDRE LURÇAT (1894–970); JOSEF HAVLÍCEK & KAREL HONZÍK (1899–1961, 1900–66); BERTHOLD LUBETKIN (1901–90)

volume; form; space; light; purity

After an eclectic, Arts-and-Crafts-influenced early career, and a self-taught education that included travelling to Mount Athos and reading Nietzsche, Charles Edouard Jeanneret, or Le Corbusier as he began to style himself, moved to Paris in 1917. He brought his messianic zeal to bear on the world's artistic capital, condemning the formalism of the École des Beaux Arts and declaring war on Cubism in his 1918 manifesto, *Après le Cubisme*, which introduced the concept of Purism.

Though Cubism had engineered a revolution in the visual arts, attempts to translate its doctrines into architecture were less successful. With a rhetorical style that became his trademark, Le Corbusier appeared utterly to condemn existing movements, but in fact took much from them. Like Cubism, Purist painting presented objects in unfamiliar ways, but rather than fragmenting them, stressed their volumetric character. This underpinned Le Corbusier's definition of architecture as 'the masterly,

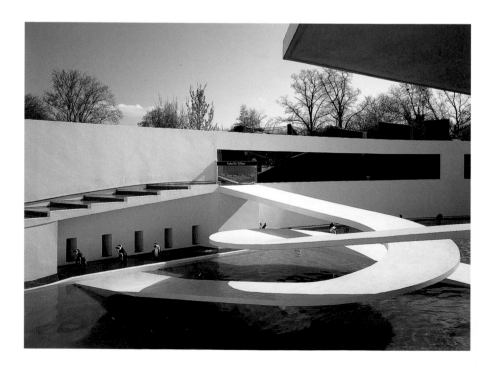

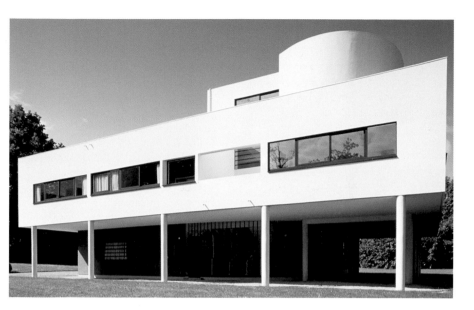

correct and magnificent play of masses brought together in light'.

In the 1920s, Le Corbusier evolved the aesthetic, indelibly connected with Modernism, of stretched white forms standing in space, which came from an appreciation of technology as well as art. New building methods, he argued, cut the relationship between structure and skin, and allowed buildings to be lifted on the ground. Roof gardens created a new relationship between nature and building, while long, horizontal windows framed views in a totally different way to conventional fenestration.

In this phase of his career, Le Corbusier shared Rationalism's confidence that industrial production would refine objects to their essential forms, making the key constituents for architectural design. His ideas continued to evolve, though, and from the 1930s onwards his work increasingly acquired a deliberate roughness, while retaining its strong sense of form.

KEY BUILDINGS

↑ Villa Savoye, Poissy, France, LE CORBUSIER, 1929–31
'A machine for living in' was Le Corbusier's definition of a house in the 1920s, and this design encapsulates many of his ideas at the time. Its Purist aesthetic is revealed in its clearly defined, subtly arranged elements, pilotis, strip windows, roof garden and the elaborate *promenade architecturale* though the interior.

← Penguin Pool, Regent's Park Zoo, London, England, BERTHOLD LUBETKIN, 1934
Strongly influenced by Le Corbusier's Purist aesthetic, with its white forms and volumes, Lubetkin also showed his heritage from Russian Constructivism in the double-helix ramp, creating the most memorable image of British Modernism.

OTHER BUILDINGS
FRANCE Maisons Laroche Jeanneret, Paris, LE CORBUSIER, 1923; Villa Stein, Garches, LE CORBUSIER, 1927; Villa Seurat, Paris, ANDRE LURÇAT, 1925–6

CZECH REPUBLIC State Pensions Office, Prague, HAVLÍCEK and HONZÍK, 1929–33

 Rationalism; Neoclassicism; Functionalism; Constructivism

 Decorative Industrialism; Expressionism; Postmodernism

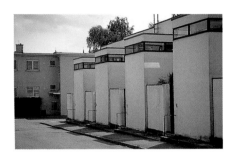

Early in the 20th century, two developments brought the relationship between architecture and Rationalism into sharp focus. Offering the possibility of constructing buildings entirely from factory-made components, Rationalism acquired a new aesthetic dimension. Meanwhile, scientific advances suggested cures to human ills, and their adoption became a moral imperative. Architectural Rationalism was one outcome of the coming together of technological progress and social commitment.

WALTER GROPIUS (1883–1969); LUDWIG MIES VAN DER ROHE (1886–1969); ERNST MAY (1886–1970); LE CORBUSIER (1887–1965); GERRIT RIETVELD (1888–1964); HANNES MEYER (1889–1954); JACOBUS JOHANNES PIETER OUD (1890–1963)

industrial production; rational plan; structure

Examples of architecture designed to improve social conditions existed from the mid-19th century, and the debate as to whether new technology demanded new forms of architecture was even older. However, it was the social turmoil that spread across Europe at the end of the First World War that fused these two trends into Rationalism. What made the rhetoric even more appealing to new regimes, whether in Soviet Russia or Social Democratic Germany, was that Rationalism thought on a big scale, and placed planning over individual buildings just as 'society' deserved precedence over 'individuals'. Architecture seemed capable of riding the back of scientific progress to bring about a new social order. The term *Neue Sachlichkeit* (new objectivity) was coined in Germany, and hints at an underlying philosophical depth to some of its best work.

Rationalism produced numerous large-scale housing developments, especially in Frankfurt and Berlin. Many had only a thin Modernist coating on traditional construction, though Ernst May at Frankfurt, and Gropius in his houses at the Weissenhofseidlung, did grapple with prefabrication and industrial production. But it was the formal power of individual buildings like Gropius's Bauhaus and the houses of Le Corbusier that stole the limelight. They provided memorable and instantly recognisable images of the 'New Architecture' and eventually eclipsed its other manifestations.

The elemental forms of Rationalism, large openings and blurring of traditional distinctions between front and back, or inside and outside, became synonymous with Modern architecture. Henry-Russell Hitchcock and Philip Johnson needed

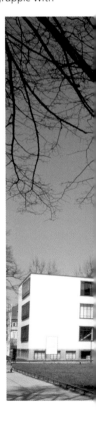

only to take the image, without the underlying social agenda, to the US for their 1932 Museum of Modern Art (MoMA) exhibition in New York, and the transformation of Rationalism from an interwoven practice of social improvement with industrial production, into an aesthetic, was complete.

KEY BUILDINGS
Houses, Weissenhofseidlung, Stuttgart, Germany, JACOBUS OUD, 1927
The Deutsche Werkbund organised the Weissenhofseidlung to demonstrate the potential of the 'New Architecture' for housing. It became a showcase for the plain and disciplined forms of Rationalism. Master-planned by Mies van der Rohe, the result belies its fraught genesis to present an apparently homogeneous construction.

Bauhaus Dessau, Germany, WALTER GROPIUS, 1926
When Gropius became head of the Bauhaus in 1919, it was located in Weimar. Political difficulties forced the move to Dessau, and gave him the opportunity to design its new home. The pinwheel plan deliberately makes all elevations equal and suggests dynamism, while the huge scale of the glass walls monumentalises the industrial techniques used to produce it.

OTHER BUILDINGS:
Barcelona Pavilion, Barcelona International Exhibition, Spain, MIES VAN DER ROHE, 1929; Schroder House, Utrecht, the Netherlands, GERRIT RIETVELD, 1924–25

 Materialism; Structural Rationalism; Corporatism

 Expressionism; Postmodernism; Totalitarianism

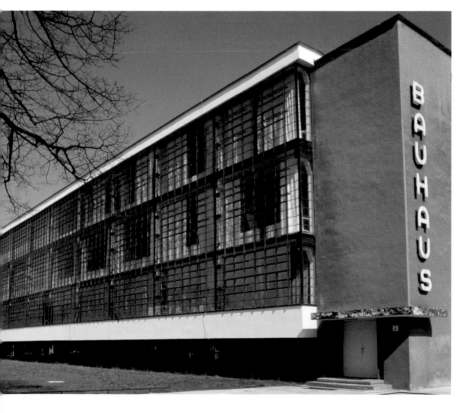

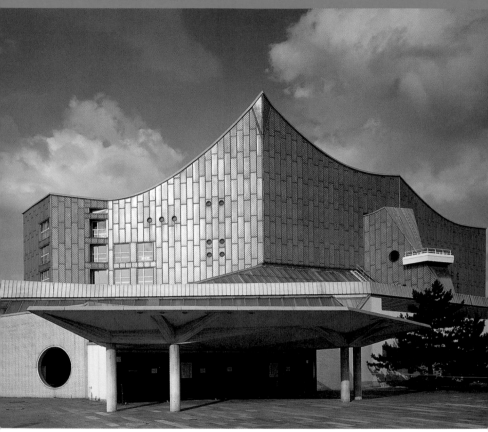

Functionalism is the belief that forms can be developed specifically to suit the functions they serve. This provided a supposedly objective base for formal invention, and suggested that architecture could derive from human needs rather than tradition or hierarchy. It quickly became, and remains, one of the most fraught aspects of Modernism and its legacy.

LOUIS SULLIVAN (1856–1924);
FRANK LLOYD WRIGHT (1867–1959);
HUGO HÄRING (1882–1958); HANS SCHAROUN
(1893–1972); ALVAR AALTO (1898–1976);
JAMES STIRLING (1924–92)

function; form; process; industrial

Although the idea that form follows function was in its element in the early Modernist experiments of the 1920s, its origins are much older. French Enlightenment architectural theorists undermined the traditional beliefs in the authority of Classical forms, while German philosopher Georg Hegel's *Aesthetics* claimed that the origins of architecture lay in providing enclosure for particular social activities, or serving function. By the middle of the 19th century, how new functions might reinvigorate architecture was as burning an issue as was the role of new materials, and was the core of teaching at the influential École des Beaux Arts.

At the end of the 1920s, Functionalism was indelibly associated with the organic free forms of architects like Hugo Häring and Hans Scharoun, who saw buildings as tools of human activity. It was this infusion of social need that took Functionalism beyond Expressionism, while its irregular and sometimes awkward forms set it in opposition to the supposed objectivity of Rationalism.

Exiled from the mainstream of Modernism, largely through disagreements with Le Corbusier, Functionalists found solace in Scandinavia. For example, the Swede Gunnar Asplund had some affinities with the local movement *Funkis*, though his work also bore elements of Neoclassicism. But in his combination of free forms and natural materials composed around human needs, the Finn Alvar Aalto demonstrated how Functionalist thinking could be more humane than Functionalism. This strand of Modernism, sometimes called the 'other tradition' in opposition to the mainstream around Le Corbusier and Mies van der Rohe, re-emerged in the 1950s and 1960s, reaching its apogee in Scharoun's Berlin Philharmonie.

The movement's most talented architects gave function a symbolic charge, vicariously bearing out Austrian philosopher Ludwig Wittgenstein's contention that 'meaning lies in use'. This inoculated their architecture against the banality to which Functionalism descended in the 1960s.

KEY BUILDINGS
Philharmonie, Berlin, Germany, HANS SCHAROUN, 1960–3
Scharoun was one of the leading advocates of Functionalism as the basis for Modern architectural form in the 1920s. In this concert hall – his masterpiece – the organisation of the auditorium to optimise acoustic quality and sightlines from every seat generates the overall form, with various tiers of seating at different levels on an irregular plan.

Town Hall, Seinäjoki, Finland, ALVAR AALTO, 1958–60
Aalto declared that 'public … and ordinary secular buildings should be in some rather mysterious harmony', revealing the symbolic and social side to his concept of Functionalism. The open ground-floor, main chamber bursting through the roof, and the relationship to his other designs in this town centre all support his concept of liberal Humanism.

OTHER BUILDINGS
Auditorium, Chicago, Illinois, US, LOUIS SULLIVAN, 1887–9; Unity Temple, Oak Park, Chicago, FRANK LLOYD WRIGHT, 1905–7; Garkau Farm, near Lübeck, Germany, HUGO HÄRING, 1924–5; Leicester University Engineering Building, England, JAMES STIRLING (with JAMES GOWAN), 1959–63

Expressionism; Constructivism

Postmodernism; Deconstructivism

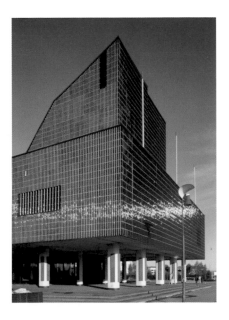

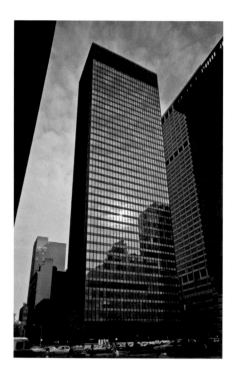

tall buildings practical as well as possible. In Chicago in particular, from the 1870s onwards, architects like William le Baron Jenney, Daniel Burnham and Louis Sullivan started to recognise that the expanded volumes and new structure changed architectural conventions out of all recognition. For Sullivan, whose essay 'The Tall Building Artistically Considered' was the first attempt to develop a theory for skyscraper design, height was 'thrilling'. He derived elegant proportions from the dimension of steelwork, and inventive ornament ultimately inspired by natural forms.

Chicago continued to attract innovative tall-building design into the 1920s. The competition for a tower for the Chicago Tribune in 1922 attracted entries from across the world – a rare point of comparison between Modernism in Europe and the US at the time. However, it was New York that became the centre of skyscraper design, with William van Alen's Chrysler Building (1930) and the Empire State Building (1931) competing for tallest structure in the world. Both support Sullivan's argument that the growth of the population, and the need for offices, would lead to larger buildings on smaller sites, which could only be achieved by going upwards. Both also express upward movement with soaring pinnacles. The Rockefeller Center explored the idea of a commercial urban quarter, mixing high- and medium-rise constructions centred around Raymond Hood's RCA Building.

After 1945, Chicago regained the lead in skyscraper design, largely through the ingenuity of architectural firm Skidmore, Owings & Merrill in reducing the amount of steel in a given structure, thus minimising cost and maximising rent. More recently, the booming economies of Asia have come to the fore, confirming the indelible link between tall buildings and corporate prosperity.

🕐 As land becomes more valuable, building high becomes more attractive. Since the late 19th century, skyscrapers have drawn on architects' ingenuity both in resolving the balance between commerce and art, and in the sheer technical and visual challenges of tall structures.

◐ WILLIAM LE BARON JENNEY (1832–1907); DANIEL BURNHAM (1846–1912); RICHARD SHREVE, WILLIAM LAMB & ARTHUR HARMON (1877–1946, 1883–1952, 1878–1958); RAYMOND HOOD (1881–1934); WILLIAM VAN ALEN (1883–1954); LUDWIG MIES VAN DER ROHE (1886–1969); WALLACE HARRISON (1895–1981); HUGH STUBBINS (1912–); CESAR PELLI (1926–)

◕ height; skyline; 'total social fact'; 'form follows finance'; phallic symbol

● Two technical developments in the second half the 19th century – the safety elevator and the steel frame – made

KEY BUILDINGS

Chrysler Building, New York, US, WILLIAM VAN ALEN, 1930
With its Jazz Age decoration, and needle-like spire with which architect and client wanted to ensure that their building would be the tallest in the world, the Chrysler Building is the essence of 1920s skyscraper design. Finished just after the Wall Street Crash undercut confidence in Capitalism, later skyscrapers would be more sober in design.

Seagram Building, New York, MIES VAN DER ROHE with PHILIP JOHNSON, 1954–8
Since arriving in the US in 1938, Mies had developed a powerful aesthetic from an incisive reading of framed construction. In the Seagram Building he attempted to convey the essence of a tall building. Often described as rational and anonymous, it is actually hauntingly ambiguous, both of its place and also universally.

OTHER BUILDINGS

US Chicago Tribune Tower, Illinoise, RAYMOND HOOD, 1925; Empire State Building, New York, SHREVE, LAMB AND HARMON, 1931; RCA Building, Rockefeller Center, New York, WALLACE HARRISON et al, 1931–40; 860–880 Lake Shore Drive, Chicago, MIES VAN DER ROHE, 1950–1; Citicorp Center, New York, HUGH STUBBINS, 1977

MALAYSIA Petronas Towers, Kuala Lumpur, CESAR PELLI, 1998

 Totalitarianism; Corporatism

 Ecoism; Regionalism

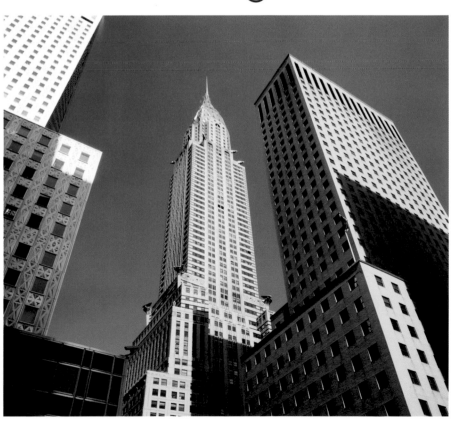

Totalitarian regimes differed from earlier political tyrannies in the extent of the technological resources they commanded, and so through the degree of control they could exercise. They had the means and motivation to orchestrate huge forces to further their authority, with results that reflect an inherent dilemma in their ideology between wanting to proclaim their technological prowess, as well as evoke historical and nationalistic references.

ALEXEI SHCHUSEV (1873–1949); **PAUL TROOST** (1879–1934); **MARCELLO PIACENTINI** (1881–1960); **LEV RUDNEV** (1885–1956); **BORIS IOFAN** (1891–1976); **GIUSEPPE TERRAGNI** (1904–43); **ALBERT SPEER** (1904–81)

power; gargantuanism; historicism; gesture

The European totalitarian regimes of the 1930s and 1940s – for example, Nazi Germany, Fascist Italy and the Soviet Union – used architecture to extend state policy. These three countries had earlier fostered important avant-gardes. How each of these regimes treated its avant-garde gives an insight into the different roles of architecture in their ideologies, and helps answer the questions posed by Totalitarianism surrounding the relationship between architecture and society in general.

In Italy, the avant-garde survived to become part of the state's official architecture. Varying interpretations of Modernism could be found in the colonies built for children of émigrés to enjoy state-sponsored holidays, as well as the Fascist Party headquarters and railway stations that sprang up across the country. The effect was to create a symbolic and operational unity through architectural patronage that the country had never previously experienced.

At best, this patronage produced Rationalist masterpieces like Giuseppe Terragni's Casa del Fascio in Como, a building that fascinates architectural intellectuals due to the rigorous complexity of its construction, detail and composition, and in challenging the 19th-century assumption that unhealthy societies produced bad architecture. But Italian Rationalism's indelible connection to Fascism provoked one survivor of the Fascist period, Ernesto Rogers, to reject Rationalism and foreshadow Regionalism in his postwar Torre Velasca in Milan.

The Nazi and Soviet regimes were more brutal to their avant-garde legacy and megalomaniac in their ambitions. Albert Speer replanned Berlin for Adolf Hitler around a gargantuan recreation of the Pantheon. Earlier, his vast Zeppelin Field in Nuremberg served as the

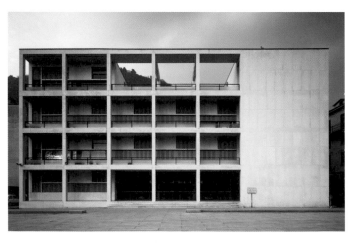

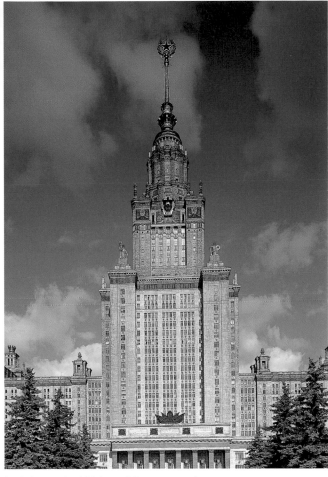

KEY BUILDINGS

← **Lomonosov University, Moscow, Russia, LEV RUDNEV, 1947–52**
Stalin secretly sent his architects to study skyscraper construction in the US, to prepare them to design the famous 'seven sister' tower blocks that proclaim Bolshevik values across Moscow and command strategic views over the city. This one contains Moscow State University in a 240-metre-tall tower flanked by four wings of student accommodation. Its decoration similarly reflects Bolshevik ideology.

←← **Casa del Fascio, Como, Italy, GIUISEPPE TERRAGNI, 1932–6**
An elegantly proportioned yet stark reinterpretation of the palazzo, this building served as offices and as a setting for Fascist rallies. Its proportions and geometries are extraordinarily sophisticated. It typifies the specific condition of Italian Rationalism, caught between an urge to modernise society as well as artistic expression, but also fascinated by history.

backdrop to Leni Riefenstahl's propaganda films, bearing out the Marxist Walter Benjamin's view that Fascism represented the extreme aestheticisation of politics.

In Russia, the rejection of Le Corbusier's design for the Palace of the Soviets in favour of a 'Stalinist wedding cake' topped by a giant statue of Lenin, marked a clear symbolic break with the avant-garde. Though some Constructivist ideas survived in urban planning, buildings acquired insipid parodies of traditional ornament.

OTHER BUILDINGS

Lenin's Mausoleum, Moscow, Russia, ALEXEI SHCHUSEV, 1924–30; House on the Embankment (apartment complex), Moscow, BORIS IOFAN, 1928–31; House of German Art, Munich, Germany, PAUL TROOST, 1933–7; Roma EUR, Italy, MARCELLO PIACENTINI et al, 1937–42; Chancellery, Berlin, Germany, ALBERT SPEER, 1938; Palace of Science and Culture, Warsaw, Poland, LEV RUDNEV, 1955

 Pre-Classicism; Monumental Urbanism, Pietism; Skyscraperism

 Rationalism; Ecoism; Regionalism

Corporatism describes the branch of architecture that emerged from the late 19th century onwards to meet the functional and aesthetic needs of large businesses. The US set the pace in corporate management and construction technology, creating possibilities for new forms of architecture to serve functional and aesthetic needs of large corporations. Although related to Functionalism and Rationalism, the specific influence of American businesses gave Corporatism a distinct character.

LOUIS SULLIVAN (1856–1924); FRANK LLOYD WRIGHT (1867–1959); ALBERT KAHN (1869–1942); LUDWIG MIES VAN DER ROHE (1886–1969); PHILIP JOHNSON (1906–2005); EERO SAARINEN (1910–61); SKIDMORE, OWINGS & MERRILL (founded 1936)

Modernism; Functionalism; management; corporate identity; industry; business; size; rationality

American architects of the 1920s, including Albert Kahn, designed factories that looked as functional as anything from the European Modern masters, and which were probably more so in operation. The following decade, Frank Lloyd Wright, who had already produced offices that reflected new principles of business organisation, designed the iconic headquarters for Johnson Wax in Wisconsin. More commonly architects followed the distinction Kahn had made between building production (for factories) and architectural representation for their headquarters. Downtown Detroit, Chicago and New York contrasted with manufacturing plants on the urban fringe in being lavishly decorated, if not downright historicist.

By presenting European Modernism's heterogeneous strands as a single unified entity, Henry-Russell Hitchcock's and Philip Johnson's 1932 Museum of Modern Art (MoMA) exhibition in New York, which defined the 'International Style', suggested that Kahn's distinction was meaningless. Corporations looking to be cultured as well as contemporary after the Depression and Second World War embraced this message. For example, Skidmore, Owings & Merrill's Lever House on Park Avenue, New York (1952) inaugurated the combination of a tower to pierce the skyline and a podium to mark a presence on the ground. At 24 storeys it was quickly overshadowed by Mies van der Rohe's Seagram Building opposite.

Soon, no North American city was complete without its steel-and-glass skyscrapers as the American economy powered its way to global hegemony. The industrial aesthetic had come to dominate corporate image, as the power of corporations began to dominate public life.

KEY BUILDINGS
→ Johnson Wax Headquarters, Racine, Wisconsin, US, FRANK LLOYD WRIGHT, 1936–9 (laboratory tower 1944–50)
Here, Wright gave each corporate function a block laid out to suit its particular needs. Each block encourages its workers to focus on their task, by turning inwards, with light coming from above. Wright also designed the furniture for the administration block. To the outside it seems a mass of red-brick forms; only later did the addition of the tower provide a focal point.

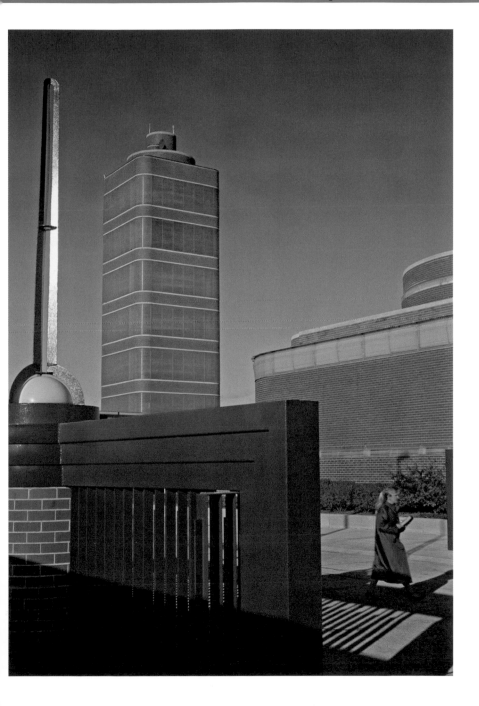

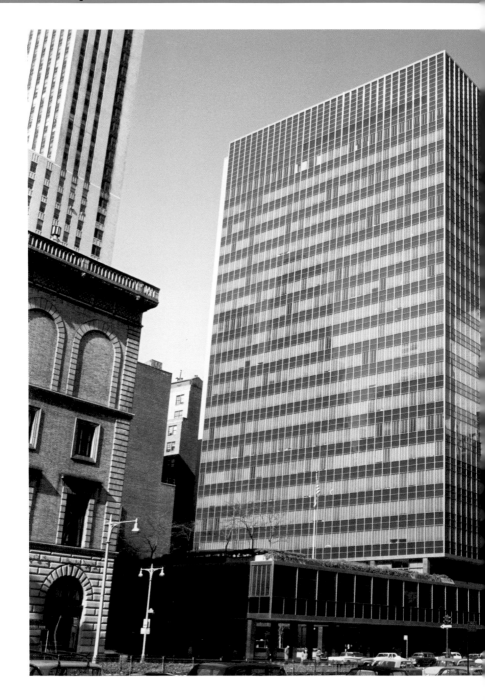

Low-rise campuses often combined research laboratories and factories, Eero Saarinen's headquarters for the tractor-maker John Deere (or his General Motors Technical Center) evocatively uniting both fact and aesthetics of function with corporate identity. In work for IBM and Mobil, US architect and industrial designer Eliot Noyes showed how corporate identity could be a tool of corporate policy. It took the global shocks of the 1970s to suggest any other relationship between business and design.

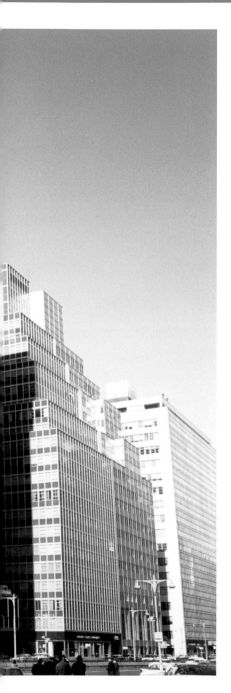

← Lever House, Park Avenue, New York, US,
SKIDMORE, OWINGS & MERRILL, 1952
This building, built for the Lever Brothers company, proved that European Modernism could adapt to corporate needs. Its clean and apparently rational design seemed to reflect commercial efficiency and openness to new technology. The idea of a tower and slab was widely copied. Later designs developed the precedent of finely dimensioned construction to co-ordinate interior layouts and furniture, to create corporate environments.

OTHER BUILDINGS
US Guaranty Building, Buffalo, New York, LOUIS SULLIVAN, 1895; Larkin Building, Buffalo, FRANK LLOYD WRIGHT, 1905; Ford Glass Factory, Detroit, Michigan, ALBERT KAHN, 1922; John Deere administration building, Moline, Illinois, EERO SAARINEN, 1957–63

 Rationalism; Usonianism; Postmodernism

 Constructivism; Ecoism

🕐 Though often applied to any unpopular architecture of the postwar period, Brutalism has more specific origins and a tighter definition. In 1954, the term 'the New Brutalism' was first applied to a group of young British architects centred around Peter and Alison Smithson, and was marked by a fascination with raw expression of materials, forms and functions.

⚫ LE CORBUSIER (1887–1965); LOUIS KAHN (1901–74); PAUL RUDOLPH (1918–97); PETER & ALISON SMITHSON (1923–2003, 1928–93); JAMES STIRLING (1924–92)

🕐 honesty; material; 'une architecture autre' (an other architecture)

⚫ Britain's massive public building programme to serve the Welfare State after the Second World War quickly adopted Modernism, but shortages of materials and a lack of knowledge meant that much of it was Modernist only in name. Inspired by the unlikely combination of German scholar Rudolf Wittkower's pioneering analyses of Renaissance architecture and the apparent rigour of new works by Le Corbusier and Mies van der Rohe, younger architects looked for a more credible intellectual base for their work. This they found by grafting an extreme application of the old doctrine of 'honesty to materials' onto the forms Mies developed for the Illinois Institute of Technology campus (1939–56). The Smithsons' Hunstanton School in Norfolk deliberately exposes all of its structure, materials and services with extraordinary clarity.

The movement's chronicler, Reyner Banham, argued that Brutalism was more 'ethic' than 'aesthetic'. It consciously sought to create an architecture that stood outside

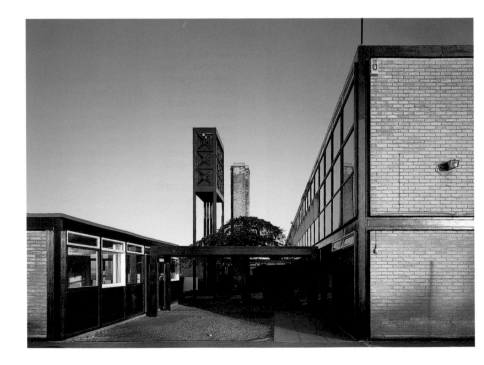

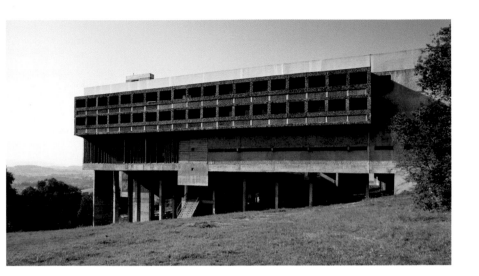

tradition and conventional canons of taste, creating its effects through unmediated materials and uncompromising forms supposedly derived from function. After Le Corbusier's use of *béton brut*, concrete was to be used in its raw state. Even detailing it to prevent weathering, still less any form of coating, was considered 'immoral', lending an emotional charge to polemical debates. It may be hard to ignore the aesthetic effect of the artful placing of windows in the Smithsons' Sugden House, or their elegantly detailed Economist Complex, but the architects would have argued that it came from the logical positioning of ordinary objects rather than specific aesthetic intent.

Brutalism had some counterparts outside the UK; for example, Paul Rudolph's concrete striations in the US. And in Sweden, in the 1950s Sigurd Lewerentz marked his return to architecture after 30 years' absence, not in his earlier, boldly Neoclassical idiom, but with materials and forms that were raw, but never crude.

KEY BUILDINGS

◀ **Hunstanton School, Norfolk, England, PETER and ALISON SMITHSON, 1949–54**
The Smithsons reduced the Rationalist aesthetic of Mies van der Rohe to a bare minimum, supposedly giving every element a basis on objective 'fact' as the starting point for an architecture that made no reference to anything other than itself or its function.

↑ **La Tourette Monastery, Eveux-sur-l'Arbresle, France, LE CORBUSIER, 1957–60**
In one of his last works, Le Corbusier explored the potential of concrete to create a variety of textures, forms and lighting conditions. In its supposedly unmediated presentation of concrete (*béton brut*), La Tourette Monstery came close to the ethos of Brutalism, the apologists of which preferred to think of it as an ethic rather than an aesthetic.

OTHER BUILDINGS
Sugden House, Watford, England, PETER and ALISON SMITHSON, 1955–6; The Economist Complex, London, England, PETER and ALISON SMITHSON, 1959–64; Flats, Ham Common, London, JAMES STIRLING (with JAMES GOWAN), 1955–8; Art and Architecture Building, Yale, New Haven, Connecticut, US, PAUL RUDOLPH, 1958–64

 Functionalism; Rationalism; Purism

 Postmodernism; Deconstructivism

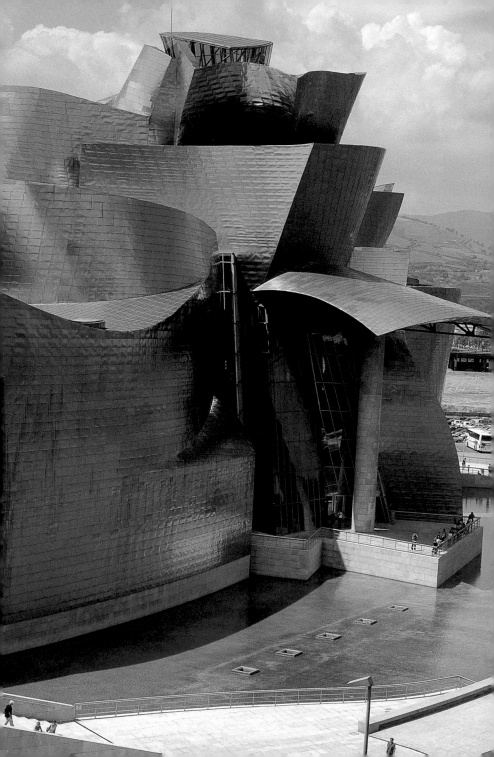

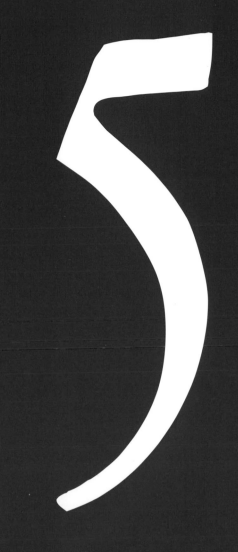

BEYOND
MODERNISM

Drawing on insights from anthropology, especially those of Claude Levi-Strauss, Structuralism proposed that underlying patterns of social relationships and human behaviour could provide a basis for architectural form that avoided the sterile and technology-driven anonymity of orthodox Modernism.

 RALPH ERSKINE (1913–95); JACOB BAKEMA (1914–81); ALDO VAN EYCK (1918–99); HERMAN HERTZBERGER (1932–)

grouping; assembly; social formation; interaction

Urban reconstruction after the Second World War seemed to give Modernism the tabula rasa it craved in order to prove its capability for creating cities. But debates over subjects like monumentality and hierarchy within the Congrès International d'Architecture Moderne, which had defined Modernist orthodoxy since its formation in 1928, quickly became controversial.

Led by architects who were too young to be active before 1939, Structuralism rejected technology as a generator of architecture and looked for archetypes that remained constant despite historical change. Its leading light was Aldo van Eyck, who had travelled across North Africa and adopted Claude Levi-Strauss's proposition that the structure of society derives from underlying networks of relationships. Operating within these social structures brought meaning and enrichment to life; being outside them was a form of exile.

Levi-Strauss adapted a concept from linguistics to anthropology. In moving the concept on to architecture, Van Eyck claimed that the task was to identify the patterns above. Though obviously requiring physical form, the shapes and spaces of a building needed to nurture rather than hinder social interaction, and its aesthetic expression was secondary. However, almost inevitably Structuralist buildings solidified what should have been flexible social structures into fixed physical ones, and their forms became recognisable images.

Van Eyck was a leading member of Team X, the younger generation of architects who brought the Congrès International d'Architecture Moderne to its knees in the 1950s. Several other members of the group, including Peter and Alison Smithson, proposed large-scale urban schemes that claimed to derive from underlying yet abstract patterns of interaction. Even Le Corbusier joined in the fun in his final project, a hospital in Venice, which had the great advantage of never being built. However, the most successful of these schemes was architectural firm Candilis-Josic-Woods's master-plan for Berlin's Frei Universität (Free University), the liberal ideals and open curriculum of which had close affinities with Structuralism.

KEY BUILDING
→ Centraal Beheer Office, Apeldoorn, the Netherlands, HERMAN HERTZBERGER, 1970–2
Hertzberger's seminal vision for a modern office broke down the space into a series of repeated small units, providing views and linkages between them, often containing communal facilities, all within an overall volume.

OTHER BUILDINGS
Orphanage, Amsterdam, the Netherlands, ALDO VAN EYCK, 1957–60; Frei Universität, Berlin, Germany, CANDILIS-JOSIC-WOODS, 1963–79; Montessori School, Delft, the Netherlands, HERMAN HERTZBERGER, 1966–70; Clare Hall College, Cambridge, England, RALPH ERSKINE, 1967; Psychiatric Hospital, Middelharnis, the Netherlands, JACOB BAKEMA, 1973–4

 Regionalism; Ecoism; Constructivism; Brutalism; Metabolism

 Rationalism; Postmodernism

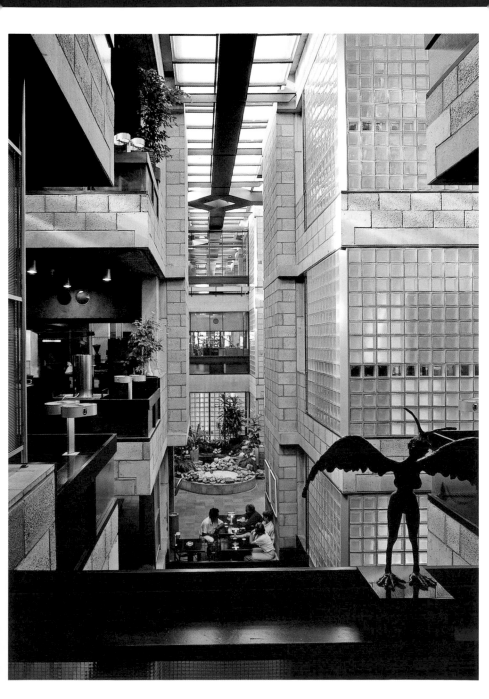

Regionalism was a reaction to Modernism's uniformity despite enormous climatic and social differences. Though by definition it varies according to location, what links Regionalism's manifestations into a coherent tendency, if not a formal movement, is the common commitment to designs that respond to local conditions, often drawing on indigenous traditions as well as Modernism.

HASSAN FATHY (1900–89); LUIS BARRAGÁN (1902–88); BRUCE GOFF (1904–82); OSCAR NIEMEYER (1907–); ERNESTO ROGERS (1909–69); GEOFFREY BAWA (1919–2003); CHARLES CORREA (1930–); RAJ REWAL (1934–)

appropriate technology; reinterpretation; adaptation; place

As Modernism became the architecture of choice across the West, it was soon apparent that however universally applicable its progressive qualities, the materials, forms and construction techniques its progenitors used were less transferable. Le Corbusier faced these challenges in the new city of Chandigarh, India, where, with his collaborators Max Fry and Jane Drew, he realised that the Indian climate as much as its construction industry necessitated adaptation.

Numerous other architects, from the ebullient and eclectic Bruce Goff in Oklahoma to the exquisitely sensitive Geoffrey Bawa in Sri Lanka, found their own way of incorporating some Modernist formal principles using local materials

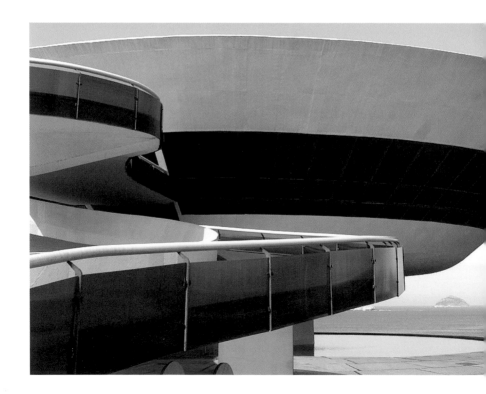

and with references to indigenous traditions. The architectural critic Kenneth Frampton's widely read essay 'Towards a Critical Regionalism' retrospectively recognised a tendency that had begun decades earlier, but offered theoretical legitimacy to mediate Modernist aims through local conditions such as climate, light and topography.

Regionalism has flourished especially where a critical stance to international Modernism has a political purpose, such as in Latin America and India. The work of Luis Barragán in Mexico, and Oscar Niemeyer in Brazil, both represent lively variants on Modernism, backed in both cases by innovative engineering that helped to produce extraordinarily dynamic forms and zestful colour schemes that are at least

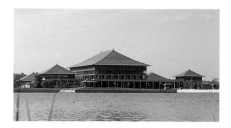

as specific to their national traditions as to anything from the Bauhaus.

Indian architecture is outwardly less spectacular. For practitioners like Charles Correa and Raj Rewal, heritage is important but unrecoverable. It offers analogies rather than models for copying, whereas Modernism suggests social goals that were not present in traditional Indian architecture. Their work is a subtle distillation of both idioms.

KEY BUILDINGS

↑ Parliament Building, Kotte (outside Colombo), Sri Lanka, GEOFFREY BAWA, 1979–82
Conceived as an island complex with an axial relationship to central Colombo, this postcolonial monument is typical of Regionalism in incorporating local concepts of space and materials within a framework that owes much to Modernism.

← Niteroi Museum of Contemporary Art, Rio de Janeiro, Brazil, OSCAR NIEMEYER, 1991–6
Largely through Niemeyer's extraordinarily long career, Brazil has developed its own lively tradition of Modernism. A common theme is his inventive use of concrete structures, here supporting a spaceship-like form that seems poised to skim across the bay.

OTHER BUILDINGS

New Gourna, near Luxor, Egypt, HASSAN FATHY, 1948; Palace of Industry exhibition building, São Paulo, Brazil, OSCAR NIEMEYER, 1951–4; Torre Velasca, Milan, Italy, ERNESTO ROGERS, 1954–8; Gandhi Ashram Museum, Ahmedabad, India, CHARLES CORREA, 1963; Los Clubes, Mexico City, Mexico, LUIS BARRAGÁN, 1967–8

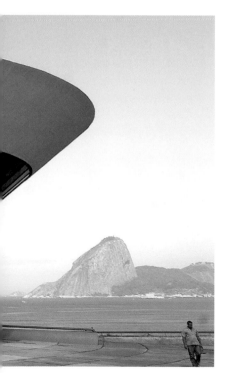

 Ecoism; Structuralism

 Metarationalism; Corporatism

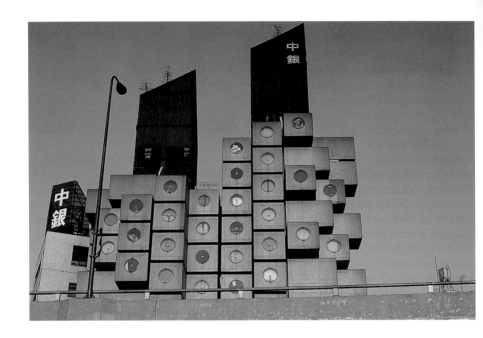

Established in 1960, the Metabolists were a talented and intellectually powerful group of Japanese architects who came to maturity in the immediate aftermath of the Second World War. The focus of the group reflected and responded to the concerns of a society undergoing rapid economic growth and technological change, and in acting as a group they provided a platform from which Japanese architecture in general could have international influence.

KENZO TANGE (1913–2005); FUMIHIKO MAKI (1928–); KIYONORI KIKUTAKE (1928–); KISHO KUROKAWA (1934–)

symbiosis; communication; technology; information

Modernism had a long history as well as several distinguished practitioners in Japan, but during the 1950s the legacy of

Japanese tradition and rapid economic expansion helped to shape a decisive break with its European roots. Kenzo Tange, who became an éminence grise of Metabolism, tried to incorporate the essence of Japanese tradition within his architecture, referring to it by analogy rather than literal copying. Another important influence was the late work of Le Corbusier, such as the Philips Pavilion at the Brussels World Fair of 1958, a heroic, sweeping form generated on mathematical principles.

But it was the emergence of consumer electronics that prompted the Metabolists to form themselves into a group at the Tokyo World Conference of Design in 1960. Starting with transistor radios and continuing in the present day with interactive mobile phones, electronic gadgets, the Metabolists argued, totally altered the distinction between public and private zones. It was possible to listen to the radio anywhere, and to engage in private activity in full public view. This, they believed, had profound implications for homes, which they envisaged as technology-laden capsules; public institutions, which they saw as networks and nodes; and cities, which they saw as playgrounds for new experiences. Their graphic imagery owed much to science fiction.

The Osaka World Fair of 1970 brought Japanese economic prowess and the Metabolists to world attention, but by then the group had begun to diverge. Never formally a member, Arata Isozaki looked to elemental, Platonic forms as ordering devices in an electronic sea. However, the relationship between the virtual and real realms remains a central concern of Japanese architecture.

OTHER BUILDINGS
JAPAN Sky House, Tokyo, KIYONORI KIKUTAKE, 1959; Rissho University, Kumagaya, FUMIHIKO MAKI, 1967–8; Sony Tower, Osaka, KISHO KUROKAWA, 1976

 Technoism; Brutalism; Structuralism; Regionalism

 Postmodernism; Neoclassicism

KEY BUILDINGS
Nagakin Capsule Tower, Tokyo, Japan, KISHO KUROKAWA, 1972
Mass technology would, the Metabolists thought, mean that private spaces could be paired down to heavily serviced 'pods', like the individual capsules in this tower block. They would be connected by means of communication and transport, which made up the public areas of the city.

▶ City Hall, Tokyo, Japan, KENZO TANGE, 1991
Tange was the most influential Japanese architect of the second half of the 20th century, and his ideas strongly influenced Metabolism. This late work displays many of his concerns with bold forms and the use of technology. More than 200 metres tall, the twin towers are among the tallest in Tokyo. By making public space at the top, the building recaptures some of the Metabolists' hopes that technology would reconfigure the relationship between public and private realms.

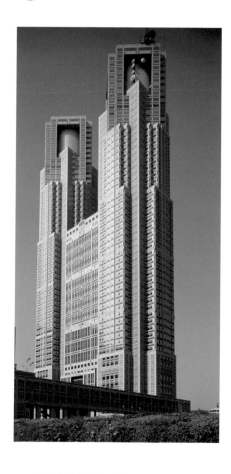

When applied to architecture, Postmodernism refers to various trends from the 1960s onwards that sought to broaden the range of reference and meaning architecture could convey, and that Modernist orthodoxy seemed to stifle. Its sources varied from pure historical reference to popular culture, but what bound these trends together was a commitment to pluralism in form and meaning. In some guises Postmodernism began to set out how architecture could re-engage with place, tradition and community.

CHARLES MOORE (1925–94); **ROBERT VENTURI** (1925–); **DENISE SCOTT BROWN** (1931–); **JAMES STIRLING** (1926–92); **MICHAEL GRAVES** (1934–); **HANS HOLLEIN** (1934–); **TERRY FARRELL** (1938–); **ROBERT STERN** (1939–); **JOHN OUTRAM** (1934–); **LEON KRIER** (1946–)

syntax; ambiguity; reference; irony; pluralism; 'both-and'; symbolism

Modernism became the dominant global architectural force after the Second World War, which exposed its limitations in dealing with context and creating meaning. Postmodernism was a specific response to this from within architectural circles, though as a criticism of Modernism it had some affinity with the political and community-based eruptions of dissatisfaction that emerged at the same time.

Robert Venturi was Postmodernism's first and most erudite exponent. In two seminal works, the book *Complexity and Contradiction* (1966) and his mother's house in Philadelphia (1965), he proposed and achieved an architecture rich in symbolism, layering, ambiguity and allusion, supporting his case with references to history and literary criticism. As a student of Louis Kahn, Venturi sought to direct Modernism away from what he saw as the banalities of corporate Modernism towards an engagement with tradition and meaning, rather than overthrow it entirely. This set the pattern for Postmodernism in the US, where the difference between Modernism and 'pomo' often came down to the cladding system, as in Philip Johnson's Corporatist AT&T tower or numerous examples by Michael Graves.

In Europe, where Modernism was as much a manifestation of social democratic

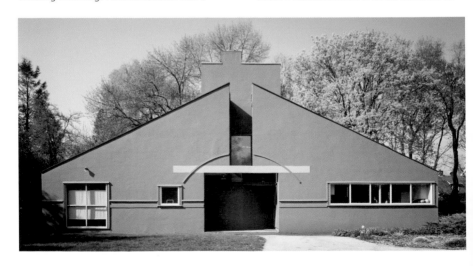

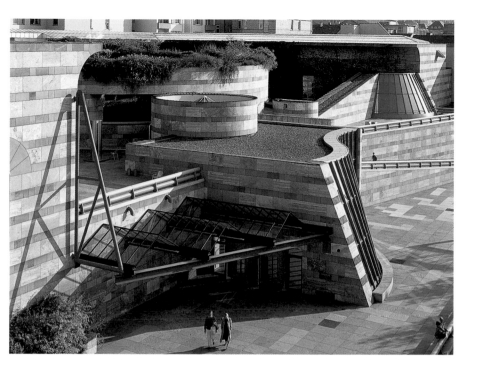

politics as of commerce, Postmodernism has a different twist. Prince Charles's advisor, Leon Krier, saw Modernism entirely as an aberration that destroyed communities. Aldo Rossi looked to the underlying patterns of urban form as the only relevant basis for architecture – engaging with tradition but not making overt reference. And the licence to refer to tradition liberated James Stirling's monumental sense of form.

↑ Staatsgalerie, Stuttgart, Germany, JAMES STIRLING, 1977–84

Stripped Neoclassical references, such as the cornice, confirm Stirling's monumental tendencies, but this is monumentality after Modernism. The gaudy colours suggest a populist element to the complex mix of cultural references, while at the basement level some pieces of wall are scattered on the ground, as if punched out, to reveal that behind all the formality of the stonework there is a Modernist steel frame.

KEY BUILDINGS

– **Vanna Venturi House, Chestnut Hill, Philidelphia, Pennsylvania, US, ROBERT VENTURI, 1964**

In this design, Venturi showed that even a small house could be rich in meaning, reference and symbolism. The chimney is an age-old symbol of domesticity; the triangular effect of the roof pitch recalls a Classical pediment, and the balanced asymmetry of the windows is a Modernist – even Constructivist – device. The inlaid arch symbolically reunites the deliberately split pediment, yet also emphasises it cleavage.

OTHER BUILDINGS

Schullin Jewellery Shop, Vienna, Austria, HANS HOLLEIN, 1972–4; Piazza d'Italia, New Orleans, Louisiana, US, CHARLES MOORE, 1979; Hotels for Disney, Florida, US, MICHAEL GRAVES, 1987–90; Disney Headquarters, California, US, MICHAEL GRAVES, 1988–90; Pumping Station, Isle of Dogs, London, JOHN OUTRAM, 1988

Baroque; Neo-Rationalism

Corporatism; Technoism; Rationalism

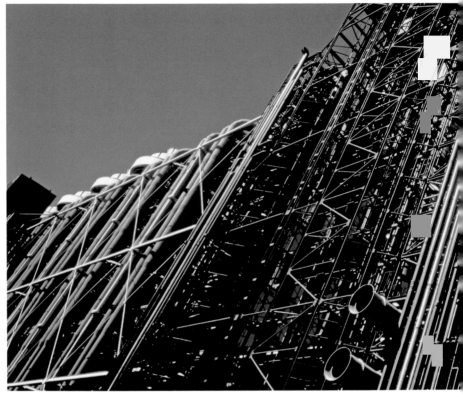

The combination of science-fiction graphics and the growing availability of consumer gadgets in the 1950s changed the relationship between architecture and technology in this period. Technoism describes how architects tried to bridge the gap between fantasy images and the real possibilities that new technology offered.

RICHARD BUCKMINSTER FULLER (1895–1983); CHARLES & RAY EAMES (1907–78, 1912–88); RON HERRON (1930–94); RICHARD ROGERS (1933–); CEDRIC PRICE (1934–2003); NORMAN FOSTER (1935–); MICHAEL HOPKINS (1935–); PETER COOK (1936–); RENZO PIANO (1937–); NICHOLAS GRIMSHAW (1938–)

technology; lightness; efficiency; frame

In 1960, the British architectural critic Reyner Banham warned architects that embracing technology meant throwing off the 'baggage', even of the recent past. Modernism, he argued, had become mired in an unhealthy and almost historicist obsession with form and composition, just when motor cars and Magimixes were there to liberate individuals from social hierarchies and debilitating traditions.

Banham's thinking found several outlets. One such outlet was the original and almost unclassifiable Cedric Price who, motivated by political commitment as much as technology, saw architectural projects as opportunities specific to their place and time that could facilitate the reordering of society.

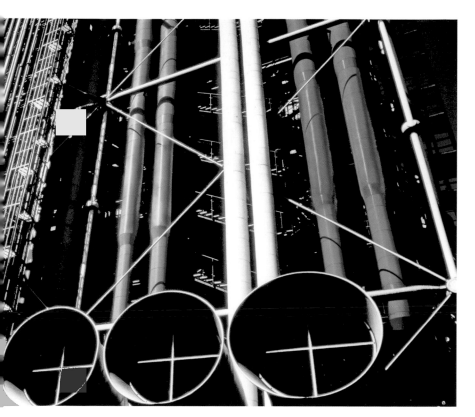

With tantalisingly industrial imagery he and theatre director Joan Littlewood proposed a Fun Palace that reconfigured performance conventions, while his Potteries Thinkbelt offered a vision of higher education as a tool for urban regeneration and social renewal. Neither was built.

Equally influential through their teaching and graphic art – though similarly thwarted in their attempts to build – was the Archigram Group, whose seductive imagery and clear affinities with the swinging sixties seemed to indicate an architecture of new possibilities.

Banham's technophilia, coupled with his enthusiasm for the Californian Case Study houses, also helped to shape the high-tech architecture of early work by Richard Rogers and Norman Foster. Foster was more literally technophilic and deeply influenced by the American Buckminster Fuller. For Rogers, technology was a means to two ends: individual fulfilment, and as a mark of breaking with tradition and convention. For all their technical imagery, creations such as the Lloyds Building in London were, in effect, hand made, displaying a dichotomy as incongruous as that between fantasy imagery and the reality of consumer gadgetry that launched Technoism in the first place.

KEY BUILDINGS

←← Centre Georges Pompidou, Paris, France,
RENZO PIANO and RICHARD ROGERS, 1971–7
Piano and Rogers won the competition for an arts centre
with a radical vision that claimed to 'democratise' access
to art. It has a series of floors free of columns or walls,
thus objects, books or studios could be placed
anywhere. This required considerable structural
gymnastics, while the services needed to cool, heat and
light the busy spaces were placed at the back and given
monumental expression.

→ Sainsbury Centre, University of East Anglia,
Norwich, England, NORMAN FOSTER, 1978
Turning the structure and, increasingly, the services such
as plumbing and ventilation into expressive forms was the
raison d'être of British 'high tech'. In this arts centre-
cum-aircraft hangar, the structure and services share a
zone defined by the steelwork, modifying the light and
temperature from outside to make it suitable for art
objects.

OTHER BUILDINGS

UK Lloyds Building, London, RICHARD ROGERS,
1978–86; Inmos Factory, Newport, South Wales,
RICHARD ROGERS, 1980–82; Schlumberger
Laboratories, Cambridge, MICHAEL HOPKINS, 1985;
Imagination Headquarters, London, RON HERRON, 1990

US Eames House, Los Angeles, California, CHARLES and
RAY EAMES, 1949

CANADA US Pavilion (geodesic dome), Montreal
World's Fair, Quebec, RICHARD BUCKMINSTER FULLER,
1967

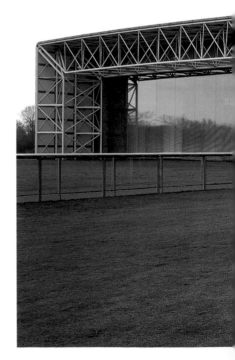

 Metabolism; Rationalism;
Ecoism

 Postmodernism; Regionalism

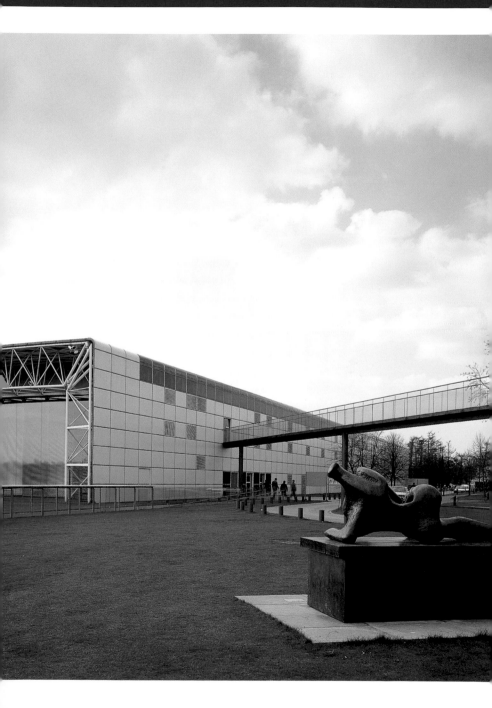

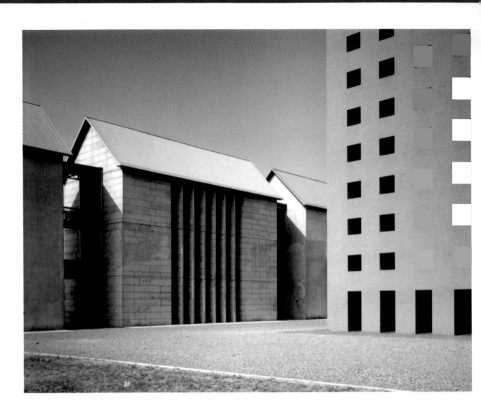

Neo-Rationalism differs from its earlier counterparts in believing the basis for architecture lies in understanding the patterns of traditional European cities rather than structure or abstract form. The development of these cities, it is argued, evolves around underlying and more or less permanent shapes that persist even when their function changes. As conveyers of cultural ideas and values, these pared-down forms become the essential elements of new designs.

OSWALD UNGERS (1926–); **ALDO ROSSI** (1931–97); **ALVARO SIZA** (1933–); **MARIO BOTTA** (1943–)

city; type; history; form

Neo-Rationalism emerged in the 1960s, centred around the need to re-engage with the legacy of historic cities, especially those in continental Europe, which had escaped the ravages of Industrialism and war. Its practitioners rejected Modernist concepts of urban form, and instead proposed that the entire fabric of a city – its streets and ordinary buildings, as well as its monuments – are essential to its character. As these elements evolve over time, they harden into forms that persist, whatever their function, and become embedded within a collective subconscious.

For two of the most sophisticated Neo-Rationalists, the German Oswald Ungers and the Italian Aldo Rossi, these forms provide analogies with the past, and their designs re-use and reinterpret them as abstract essences, rather than models to be copied exactly.

Rossi was strongly influenced by Giorgio de Chirico's paintings, and his buildings have a haunting sparseness as if their forms are trying to speak, but lack the capability to do so. What they might say seems to come from the very essence of their cultural tradition, and their inability to say it quickly passes from poignancy to tragedy. Neo-Rationalists see this condition as an inevitable result of a wider cultural crisis following the alienation of Capitalism and the catastrophes of Nazism and Soviet Communism. Their architectural theories draw widely on social and political concepts.

To overcome this disjunction, Rossi adopted some aspects of Surrealism, playing with form and scale in the design of teapots that resemble buildings, and buildings whose scale is impossible to calibrate. For Ungers, the grid is constant, underlying an abstract ordering device that brings coherence to the assembly of forms.

KEY BUILDINGS

← San Cataldo Cemetery, Modena, Italy, ALDO ROSSI, from 1980

Rossi's haunting vision treats a cemetery as a city of the dead. For Rossi, a city is a collection of archetypal forms that have persisted and evolved through history. Here, the monuments are the red-coloured ossuary and a crematorium chimney, with human remains placed, like the homes of the living, in plain buildings on arcaded streets.

↓ Galician Centre for Contemporary Art, Santiago de Compostella, Spain, ALVARO SIZA, 1988–93

An apparently simple form gradually reveals extraordinary complexity, generated by responses to the history of the site, the neighbouring monuments and street pattern. As well as a museum, the building acts as a meditation on the city, its history and culture.

OTHER BUILDINGS

Ungers House, Cologne, Germany, OSWALD UNGERS, 1959; Gallaretese Housing, Milan, Italy, ALDO ROSSI, 1970–3; School at Morbio Inferiore, Switzerland, MARIO BOTTA, 1972–07; Church of Santa Maria de Canaveses, Oporto, Portugal, ALVARO SIZA, 1990–6

 Rationalism; Neoclassicism; Sublimism

 Technoism; Ecoism

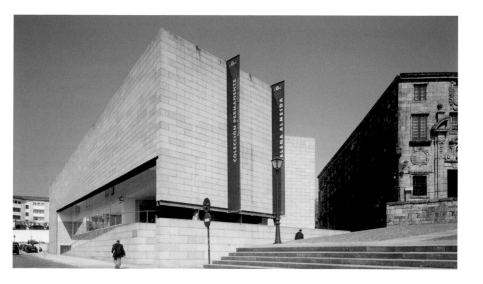

Deconstructivism, an ungainly combination of Constructivism and Jacques Derrida's literary concept of deconstruction, tried to identify common ground between a new formal inventiveness and attempts to diversify the theoretical base of architecture. Both trends emerged in the 1980s in response to the evident shortcomings and eventual collapse of Modernist conventions.

GÜNTER BEHNISCH (1922–); FRANK GEHRY (1929–); PETER EISENMAN (1932–); BERNARD TSCHUMI (1944–); HELMUT SWICZINSKY (1944–); ZAHA HADID (1950–); WOLF PRIX (1942–)

language; meaning; negativity

Changing economic policies and a wave of new theoretical ideas made architecture more diverse in the 1980s than it had been for a generation. Both the outward forms and intellectual content of architecture demonstrated this diversity. Taboos on looking at architecture of the past were lifted as architectural history became a catalogue of motifs, while more theoretically

inclined architects looked to contemporary intellectual developments – in particular French Post-Structuralism – where they found analogies to their intentions of overturning Modernist orthodoxy.

One of the 'discoveries' from architectural history was Russian Constructivism. This had two great attractions. First, having received only scant attention in the history of Modernism, it was possible to overlook its origins in fierce debates about the role of architecture in society and see its formal inventiveness as evidence of creative freedom, even to the extent of implying that architecture was an autonomous discipline. Second, because it came out of Modernism, albeit a slightly recherché corner of the canon, it was an antidote to Postmodernism and thus became a proxy that allowed a surrogate ideological war to continue.

Meanwhile, investigations of the syntax of Modernism started to draw on Derrida's Post-Structuralist linguistics. Although attempts to apply Deconstruction directly to architecture were never entirely successful, it did provide a series of terms, such as

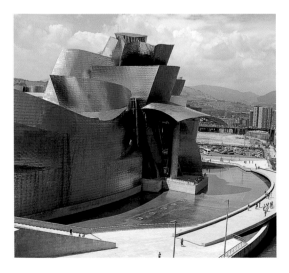

'différance', which seemed to be applicable to architecture's intellectual soup. An exhibition on Deconstructivism at the Museum of Modern Art (MoMA) in 1988 tried to make these connections explicit, though perhaps served to show up the inherent instability of the position. But what could not be foreseen was that information technology (IT) was on the verge of an explosion that would make possible the building of the visionary forms of the exhibition's featured architects. By the new millennium, the term Deconstructivism was all but buried under the drama of extraordinary forms.

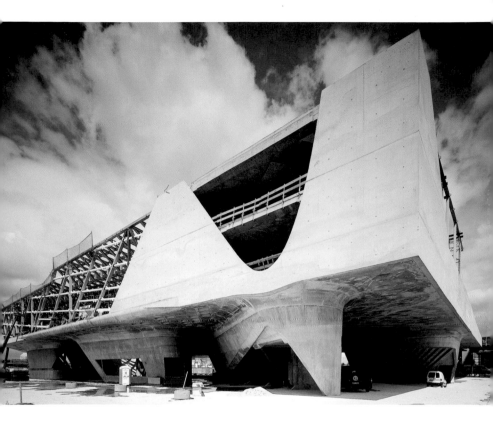

KEY BUILDINGS

◄ **Guggenheim Museum, Bilbao, Spain,**
FRANK GEHRY, 1997
Gehry rewrote all manner of architectural convention in the world's most famous new building of the 1990s. Using computer programs developed for fighter jets, he evolved the complex, titanium-clad forms, while the structure occupies an awkward zone between the outer shell and the inner gallery spaces.

↑ **Science Centre, Wolfsburg, Germany,**
ZAHA HADID, 2005
Hadid's career subsequent to appearing in the MoMA exhibition in 1988 demonstrates both the strengths and weaknesses of Deconstructivist architecture. The formal inventiveness is still there. However, rather than justifying them by flimsy analogy with esoteric literary theory, in recent works the forms derive from complex mathematics, and can now be analysed and built thanks to massive computing power.

OTHER BUILDINGS

Parc de la Villette, Paris, France, BERNARD TSCHUMI, 1982–93; Wexner Center, University of Ohio, Athens, Ohio, US, BERNARD TSCHUMI, 1990; Attic Conversion, Vienna, Austria, WOLF PRIX and HELMUT SWICZINSKY, 1984–8; Hysolar Building, University of Stuttgart, Germany, GÜNTER BEHNISCH, 1988; Vitra Fire Station, Weil-am-Rhein, Germany, ZAHA HADID, 1994

 Constructivism; Metarationalism; Technoism

 Postmodernism; Purism

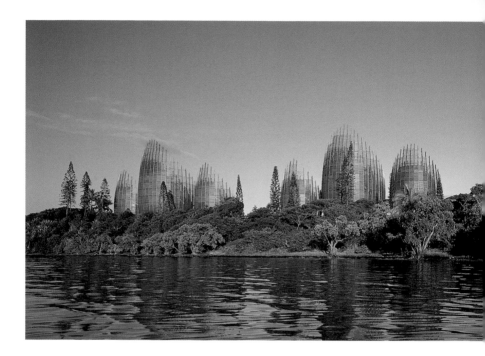

Ecoism is where the exponents of 'high tech' migrated after suspicions grew that technology on its own cannot generate form. Sustainability, by contrast, offers an unassailable moral imperative that can justify revolutionary approaches to the form and use of materials, often by using computer simulations to inform the design process.

EDWARD CULLINAN (1933–); NORMAN FOSTER (1935–); MICHAEL HOPKINS (1935–); RICK MATHER (1937–); RENZO PIANO (1937–); IAN RITCHIE (1947–)

sustainability; conservation; innovation

Rather as Structural Rationalism used mathematical principles to provide an objective reason for particular architectural forms, Ecoism seeks a rationale for design innovation in principles of sustainability, a task that global warming makes urgent.

In the past, this rationale came from experience: vernacular buildings, using local skills and materials, and whose form was closely adapted to their environments, are inherently more sustainable than those with an alien aesthetic that use unfamiliar materials. However, computer imaging can now accurately predict a building's performance and study the effects of even minute design changes. Thus designers can ensure their designs have the most advantageous form, orientation and finish for particular activities on particular sites.

Sustainability demands a holistic approach to given physical conditions, from climatic conditions such as latitude, rainfall and prevailing winds, to the micro level of individual details. It also requires an appreciation of how these factors relate to the building's function. Aesthetic effects vary

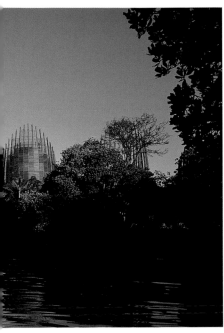

KEY BUILDINGS

← Jean-Marie Tjibaou Cultural Center, Nouméa, New Caledonia, RENZO PIANO, 1991–8
Built to celebrate the local Kanak culture, this design comprising 10 shell-like timber forms is an attempt to match local traditions and materials with Western technological know-how – a more responsive approach than globalisation.

↓ Office Building, Stockley Park, London, England, IAN RITCHIE, 1990
With giant solar shading and specially treated glazed walls, Ritchie here attempted to show that a building that meets the image and expectation of modern businesses need not be wasteful of natural resources.

OTHER BUILDINGS

UK Portcullis House, London, MICHAEL HOPKINS, 1989–2000; Student Residence, East Anglia University, Norwich, RICK MATHER, 1991; Archeolink Visitor Centre, Aberdeenshire, EDWARD CULLINAN, 1995; 30 St Mary Axe, London (Swiss Re Tower – the 'Gherkin'), NORMAN FOSTER, 2004

widely too, and can be counter-intuitive. With double and triple skins of glass to act as buffers and channels for excess heat, even greenhouses might not be energy profligate, while floor slabs and structure can be used to absorb surplus heat and emit it in colder conditions.

Occasionally, architects take advantage of the ability to manipulate a building's entire shape into an unusual form, which can improve natural ventilation or daylight. However, on an urban site, for instance, the building's form may be fixed, and improving the performance of an otherwise conventional building might then need to come from the addition of, for example, external flues and chimneys to facilitate air movement across it. Other gestures might be invisible yet still have an effect, raising the extent to which the experience of architecture is visual or dependent on other stimuli.

 Regionalism; Technoism

 Corporatism; Rationalism; Postmodernism

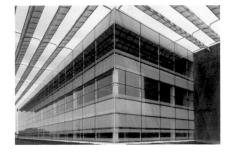

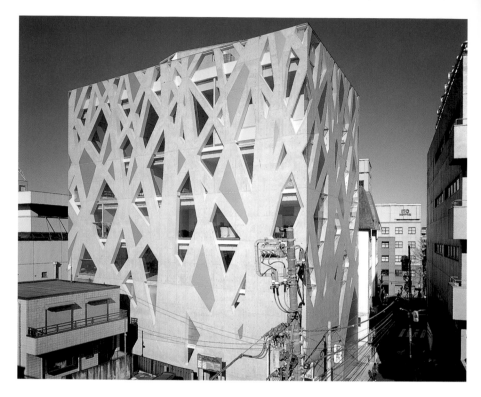

 Metarationalism is what happens to architecture when the logic of economist James Galbraith's view that in the affluent society there is no meaningful distinction between luxury and necessity meets that of complexity science with its ability to overturn conventional structural logic. The result is a feast of consumerist experiences presented within phenomenally complex forms.

TOYO ITO (1941–); REM KOOLHAAS (1944–); DANIEL LIBESKIND (1946–); STEVEN HOLL (1947–); JACQUES HERZOG & PIERRE DE MEURON (both 1950–); PETER DAVIDSON & DON BATES (1955–, 1953–); WINY MAAS, JACOB VAN RIJS & NATHALIE DE VRIES (1959–, 1964–, 1965–); ALEJANDRO ZAERA-POLO & FARSHID MOUSSAVI (1963–, 1965–)

IT; variance; fractal; folding; warping

Rem Koolhaas' *Delirious New York* almost managed to prove that eating oysters, naked apart from boxing gloves, on the ninth floor of Manhattan's Downtown Athletic Club was a logical activity for metropolitan bachelors. Late Capitalism combined with Surrealism and the influence of film to set the terms of a new reality. This might have been relative and unstable, but then, argued Koolhaas, so was Modernism itself.

This is the logic of Metarationalism, which has its roots in consumerism, both in the way mass affluence overturns economic relations and the spatial configuration of cities, and consumer electronics change how we perceive our surroundings. Modernism was but one step in an ongoing process, and whatever its formal power, trying to recreate it is useless sentimentality. Society, if not architecture, will make any meaning its forms may have had obsolete.

Koolhaas talks about the restrictions of the 'zebra', the rigid division of buildings into alternating strips of space and structure, and seeks to splinter the layers into folded surfaces. They can, but do not have to respond to function. Toyo Ito's Sendai Mediatheque in Miyagi, Japan (1995–2000) does something similar to the vertical structure. Rather than solid columns it has towers of twisted steel tubes that allow people, data and energy to pass through without distinguishing between them.

As the point where aesthetics is consummated into an economic relationship, shopping is the fundamental Metarationalist activity. Increasingly, boutiques acquire the iconic status of art galleries, and the objects inside them are treated as if they might be interchangeable. In a final twist of relativism, it is the setting that determines whether a piece of fabric is art or clothing, or a piece of metal is jewellery or sculpture.

KEY BUILDINGS

Tods Store, Tokyo, Japan, TOYO ITO, 2004
High-quality boutiques have become vehicles for avant-garde design. Here, Ito shows his interest in using structure driven by complexity science rather than Newtonian physics to define a field of spatial experiences.

Congrexpo (Lille Grand Palais), Lille, France, REM KOOLHAAS/OFFICE FOR METROPOLITAN ARCHITECTURE (OMA), 1994
A giant exhibition hall and congress centre associated with the Channel Tunnel rail link, Congrexpo demonstrated OMA founder Rem Koolhaas's ideas about bigness, a condition he argued rendered traditional architectural concepts obsolete. Vast spaces are differentiated only by association, and the distance from perimeter to centre is too great for the facade to reveal internal activity.

OTHER BUILDINGS
Yokohama Ferry Terminal, Japan, FOREIGN OFFICE ARCHITECTS (ALEJANDRO ZAERA-POLO and FARSHID MOUSSAVI), 2002; Federation Square, Melbourne, LAB ARCHITECTURE (PETER DAVIDSON and DON BATES), 2002; Schaulager Foundation, Basle, Switzerland, HERZOG AND DE MEURON (JACQUES HERZOG and PIERRE DE MEURON), 2003; Villa VPRO, Hilversum, the Netherlands, MVRDV (WINY MASS, JACOB VAN RIJs and NATALIE DE VRIES), 1997; Jewish Museum, Berlin, Germany, DANIEL LIBESKIND, 1999; Het Oosten Office, Amsterdam, the Netherlands, STEVEN HOLL, 2000

 Deconstructivism; Rationalism; Expressionism

 Neo-Rationalism; Postmodernism; Corporatism

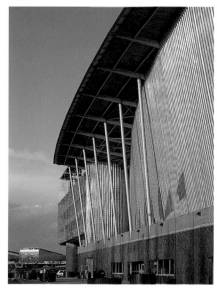

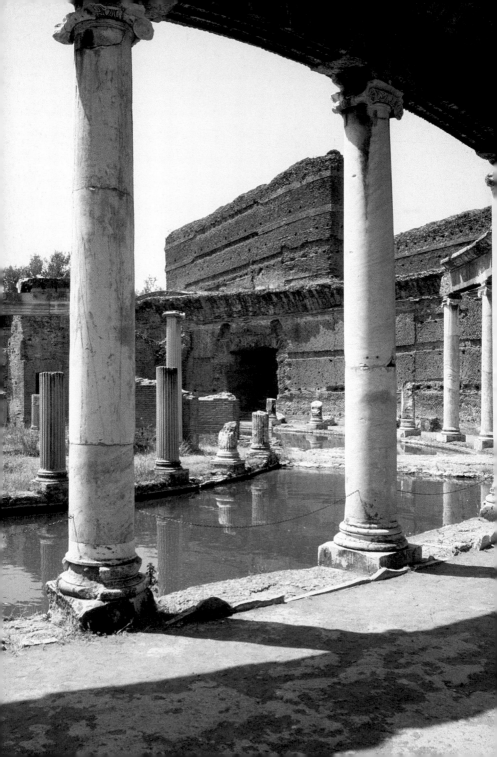

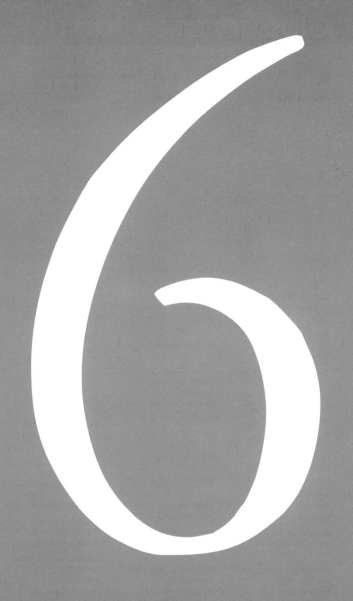

REFERENCE
SECTION

A

Abbey of St Denis,
outside Paris (1135–44)
Gothic Scholasticism

Agrigento, various temples,
Sicily (510–430 BC)
Hellenic Classicism

Al-Aqsa Mosque,
Jerusalem (AD 705)
Islamicism

Alhambra Palace,
Granada, Spain (1338–90)
Islamicism

All Hallows by the Tower,
London (1765)
Sublimism

All Saints, Margaret Street,
London (1850–59)
Medievalism

Altes Museum, Berlin
(1824–8)
Neoclassicism

Amber Palace,
Rajasthan, India (1623–68)
Indism

Amsterdam Orphanage,
Amsterdam (1957–60)
Structuralism

Amsterdam Stock Exchange,
Amsterdam (1897–1903)
Structural Rationalism

Ancy-le-Franc,
Burgandy, France (c. 1546)
Regional Classicism

Angkor Wat, Cambodia
(early 12th century)
Indo-Khmerism

Archeolink Visitor Centre,
Aberdeenshire,
Scotland (1995)
Ecoism

Arch of Titus,
Rome (AD 82)
Roman Classicism

Ashridge House,
Hertfordshire, England
(from 1808)
Exoticism

Auditorium,
Chicago (1887–9)
Functionalism

B

Bank of England,
London (1792)
Sublimism

Barcelona Pavilion,
Barcelona (1929)
Rationalism

Barrière de la Villette,
Paris (1785–9)
Sublimism

Basilica di Santa Maria del Fiore (Florence Cathedral) (from 1296;
cupola 1418–36)
Inventionism

Baths of Caracalla,
Rome (AD 211–17)
Roman Classicism

Bavinger House, Norman,
Oklahoma (1950–05)
Usonianism

Bauhaus Dessau,
Germany (1926)
Rationalism

Bedford Square,
London (1775)
Georgian Urbanism

Belvedere, Vienna
(1714–23)
Rococo

Berlin Chancellery,
Berlin (1938)
Totalitarianism

Berlin Philharmonie,
Berlin (1960–3)
Functionalism

Biblioteca Laurentiana,
Florence (1524)
Mannerism

Bibliothèque Nationale,
Paris (1860–8)
Structural Rationalism

Bibliothèque Sainte Geneviève, Paris
(1845–50)
Structural Rationalism

Blenheim Palace,
Woodstock,.Oxon, England
(1705–20)
Anglican Empiricism

Blue Mosque,
Istanbul (1610–16)
Islamicism

British Museum,
London (1823–47)
Neoclassicism

British Museum, Old Reading Room,
London (1852–7)
Materialism

Burlington House (the Royal Academy),
London (from 1717)
Palladianism

C

Canterbury Cathedral,
Canterbury, England
(1096–1185)
Gothic Scholasticism

Carson Pirie Scott department store,
Chicago (1899)
Decorative Industrialism

Casa del Fascio,
Como, Italy (1932–6)
Totalitarianism

Caserta Royal Palace,
Caserta, Italy (1751)
Absolutism

Centraal Beheer Office,
Apeldoorn, the Netherlands
(1970–2)
Structuralism

Chapel of St John, Tower of London, London
(1086–97)
Christian Classicism

Chartres Cathedral,
France (1194–1260)
Gothic Scholasticism

Chateau de Chambord,
Loire Valley, France
(1519–47)
Regional Classicism

China Pavilion,
Drottningholm,
Sweden (1760)
Exoticism

Chiswick House,
London (1725–9)
Palladianism

Christchurch Spitalfields,
London (1723–9)
Anglican Empiricism

D

Chrysler Building,
New York (1930)
Skyscraperism

Church of Santa Maria de Canaveses,
Oporto, Portugal (1990–6)
Neo-Rationalism

Citadel, Teotihuacan,
Mexico (c. AD 600)
Pre-Columbianism

Clare Hall College,
Cambridge University,
England (1967)
Structuralism

Cloth Hall, Ypres,
Belgium (1202–1304)
Gothic Commercialism

Colosseum,
Rome (AD 70–82)
Roman Classicism

Congrexpo (Lille Grand Palais), Lille, France (1994)
Metarationalism

Cordoba Mosque,
Cordoba, Spain
(AD 785–987)
Islamicism

Covent Garden Piazza,
London (1631)
Georgian Urbanism

The Crystal Palace,
London (1851)
Materialism

Cuzco, City of,
Peru (1450–1532)
Pre-Columbianism

D

Disney hotels,
Florida (1987–90)
Postmodernism

Dneprostroi Dam,
Ukraine (1932)
Constructivism

Doges Palace,
Venice (1309–1424)
Gothic Commercialism

Dome of the Rock,
Jerusalem (AD 684)
Islamicism

Dresden Opera House,
Dresden, Germany
(1838–41)
Monumental Urbanism

Durham Cathedral,
Durham, England
(1093–1132)
Christian Classicism

E

The Economist Complex,
London (1959–64)
Brutalism

Edinburgh New Town,
Edinburgh, Scotland
(from 1767)
Georgian Urbanism

Eigen Haard housing,
Amsterdam (1921)
Expressionism

Einstein Tower, Potsdam,
Germany (1917–21)
Expressionism

El Escorial,
near Madrid (1559–84)
Pietism

Empire State Building,
New York (1931)
Skyscraperism

The Erechtheion,
Athens (421–405 BC)
Hellenic Classicism

F

Fatehpur Sikri,
Agra, India (1569–80)
Indism

Federation Square,
Melbourne (2002)
Metarationalism

Floating Torii Gate,
Miyajima, Japan
(12th century)
Shintoism

Ford Glass Factory,
Detroit (1922)
Corporatism

Frei Universität,
Berlin (1963–79)
Structuralism

G

Galician Centre for
Contemporary Art,
Santiago de Compostella,
Spain (1988–93)
Neo-Rationalism

Gallaretese Housing,
Milan (1970–3)
Neo-Rationalism

Gandhi Ashram Museum,
Ahmedabad, India (1963)
Regionalism

Garkau Farm, near Lübeck,
Germany (1924–5)
Functionalism

Gate of the Sun,
Tiahuanaco, Peru
(c.1000–1200)
Pre-Columbianism

Glypothek,
Munich (1816–34)
Neoclassicism

Great Mosque,
Damascus (AD 706–15)
Islamicism

Great Pyramids of Giza,
outside Cairo
(c. 2631–2498 BC)
Pre-Classicism

Great Temple of Amon,
Karnak, Egypt
(1530–323 BC)
Pre-Classicism

Great Wall of China
(214 BC)
Confucianism

Greg Affleck House,
Bloomfield Hills, Michigan
(1941)
Usonianism

Guggenheim Museum,
Bilbao, Spain (1997)
Deconstructivism

H

Hadrian's Villa,
Tivoli, Italy (AD 124)
Roman Classicism

Hagia Sophia,
Istanbul (AD 532–7)
Christian Classicism

Het Oosten Office,
Amsterdam (2000)
Metarationalism

Holkham Hall, Norfolk,
England (from 1734)
Palladianism

Hotel de Soubise,
Paris (1737–40)
Rococo

House of German Art,
Munich (1933–7)
Totalitarianism

House of Nobles,
Stockholm (1641–74)
Regional Classicism

House on the
Embankment (apartment
complex), Moscow
(1928–31)
Totalitarianism

Houses of Parliament,
London (1835–68)
Victorianism

Humayun's Tomb,
Delhi (1585)
Indism

Hunstanton School,
Norfolk, England (1949–54)
Brutalism

I

Il Gesu, Rome (1568–84)
Pietism

Il Redentore, Venice (1576)
Mannerism

Imperial Palace, Forbidden
City, Beijing (1407–20)
Confucianism

Imperial Villa,
Katsura, Japan (1620)
Shintoism

India Arch,
New Delhi (1921–31)
Imperialism

Inmos Factory, Newport,
South Wales (1980–82)
Technoism

Ishtar Gate, Babylon,
Mesopotamia (605–563 BC)
Pre-Classicism

J

Janta Manta, Jaipur,
Rajasthan, India (1726–34)
Indism

Jean-Marie Tjibaou
Cultural Center, Nouméa,
New Caledonia (1991–8)
Ecoism

Jewish Museum,
Berlin (1999)
Deconstructivism

John Deere
administration building,
Moline, Illinois (1957–63)
Corporatism

Johnson Wax
Headquarters, Racine,
Wisconsin (1936–9)
Corporatism

K

Karlskirche, Vienna (1716)
Absolutism

Kasuga Shrine, Nara,
Japan (from AD 768)
Shintoism

Keble College, Oxford
University, England
(1868–82)
Victorianism

Khajuraho, various
temples, India (late 9th
century–11th century)
Indo-Khmerism

Kings College Chapel,
Cambridge University,
England (1446–1515)
Gothic Scholasticism

Kirby Hall,
Northamptonshire, England
(1570–02)
Regional Classicism

Kotte Parliament
Building, Sri Lanka
(1979–82)
Regionalism

Kunsthistorisches
Museum, Vienna (1869)
Monumental Urbanism

L

Lake Shore Drive (860–880), Chicago (1950–1)
Skyscraperism

La Madeleine, Paris (1806)
Neoclassicism

L'Arc de Triomphe,
Paris (1806–35)
Monumental Urbanism

La Tourette Monastery,
Eveux-sur-l'Arbresle, France (1957–60)
Brutalism

Laxmi Vilas Palace,
Baroda, India (1881–90)
Imperialism

Leicester University Engineering Building,
Leicester, England (1959–63)
Functionalism

Lenin's Mausoleum,
Moscow (1924–30)
Totalitarianism

Lever House,
New York (1952)
Corporatism

Lion Gate, Mycenae,
Greece (c. 1250 BC)
Proto-Classicism

Lloyds Building,
London (1978–86)
Technoism

Loggia dei Lanzi,
Florence (1376–82)
Inventionism

Lomonosov University,
Moscow (1947–52)
Totalitarianism

Los Clubes,
Mexico City (1967–8)
Regionalism

Louvre, east front,
Paris (1667)
Absolutism

Lovell Beach House,
Newport Beach, California (1925–6)
Usonianism

M

Machu Picchu,
near Cuzco, Peru (c. 1500)
Pre-Columbianism

Madinat-al-Zahra, City of,
near Cordoba, Spain
(AD 936)
Islamicism

Madonna di San Biagio,
Montepulciano, Italy (1519–29)
Idealism

Madras University Senate House, Madras, India (1874–9)
Imperialism

Maisons Laroche Jeanneret, Paris (1923)
Purism

Maritzhuis,
the Hague (1633–5)
Regional Classicism

Mayo College,
Rajasthan, India (1875–9)
Imperialism

Melk Monastery,
Melk, Austria (1702–14)
Rococo

Mereworth Castle,
Kent, England (1722–5)
Palladianism

Metro entrance, Porte Dauphine, Paris (1900)
Decorative Industrialism

Mexico City Cathedral,
Mexico City (1585)
Pietism

Mohenjaro-daro and Harappa, Indus Valley, India (mid-third millennium BC)
Indism

Montessori School, Delft,
the Netherlands (1966–70)
Structuralism

Monticello, Virginia (from 1769–1809)
Palladianism

Mosque of Al-Azhar,
Cairo (AD 970)
Islamicism

N

Nagakin Capsule Tower,
Tokyo (1972)
Metabolism

Natural History Museum,
Oxford, England (1854–8)
Materialism

New Gourna, near Luxor,
Egypt (1948)
Regionalism

North and South Pyramids of Seneferu,
Dahshur, Egypt (2723 BC)
Pre-Classicism

Notre Dame Cathedral,
Paris (1163–1250)
Gothic Scholasticism

Notre Dame du Raincy,
Paris (1922–3)
Structural Rationalism

O

Opera Garnier,
Paris (1861–74)
Monumental Urbanism

Oriel Chambers,
Liverpool, England (1864–5)
Materialism

Ospedale degli Innocenti,
Florence (1419–24)
Inventionism

Ottobeuren Abbey,
Ottobeuren, Germany (1744–67)
Rococo

P

Paddington Station,
London (1854)
Materialism

Pagoda, Kew Gardens,
London (1757–62)
Exoticism

Palace of King Minos,
Knossos, Crete (pre-1400 BC)
Proto-Classicism

Palais de Fontainebleu,
Seine-et-Marne,
France (1568)
Regional Classicism

Palais de Justice,
Brussels (1866–83)
Monumental Urbanism

Palais Stoclet,
Brussels (1905–11)
Decorative Industrialism

Palazzo Carignano,
Turin (1679)
Baroque

Palazzo Chiericati,
Vicenza, Italy (1549)
Mannerism

Palazzo della Cancelleria,
Rome (1486–96)
Idealism

Palazzo del Te,
Mantua, Italy (1525–35)
Mannerism

Palazzo Ducale,
Urbino, Italy (1444–82)
Humanism

Palazzo Massimo,
Rome (1532–6)
Mannerism

Palazzo Medici,
Florence (1444–59)
Inventionism

Palazzo Rezzonico,
Venice (1667)
Baroque

Palazzo Rucellai,
Florence (1446–57)
Humanism

Palm House, Kew Gardens, London (1849)
Materialism

The Pantheon,
Rome (AD 118–26)
Roman Classicism

The Panthéon,
Paris (from 1756)
Neoclassicism

Parc de la Villette,
Paris (1982–93)
Deconstructivism

Parthenon,
Athens (447–432 BC)
Hellenic Classicism

Pazzi Chapel,
Florence (1429–46)
Inventionism

Penguin Pool, Regent's
Park Zoo, London (1934)
Purism

Petronas Towers,
Kuala Lumpur (1998)
Skyscraperism

Piazza d'Italia, New
Orleans, Louisiana (1979)
Postmodernism

Piazza San Pietro,
Rome (1656)
Baroque

Place de le Concord,
Paris (1755)
Absolutism

Pommersfelden Schloss,
Germany (from 1711)
Rococo

Pompidou Centre,
Paris (1971–7)
Technoism

Portcullis House,
London (1989–2000)
Ecoism

Post Office Savings Bank,
Vienna (1904–06)
Decorative Industrialism

Preah Ko Temple, Angkor,
Cambodia (c. AD 880)
Indo-Khmerism

Pumping Station, Isle of
Dogs, London (1988)
Postmodernism

Pyramid of the Sun,
Teotihuacán, Mexico
(c. AD 250)
Pre-Columbianism

Q

Qutb Minar, Delhi (1199)
Indism

R

Rajarajeshvara Temple,
India (late 9th century
–11th century)
Indo-Khmerism

RCA Building, Rockefeller
Center, New York
(1931–40)
Skyscraperism

The Red House,
Bexleyheath, England
(1859)
Anti-Urbanism

Regent's Park,
London (from 1811)
Georgian Urbanism

Rheims Cathedral,
Rheims, France (1211–90)
Gothic Scholasticism

Rissho University,
Kumagaya, Japan (1967–8)
Metabolism

Robie House,
Chicago (1909)
Anti-Urbanism

Roma EUR,
Rome (1937–42)
Totalitarianism

Royal Courts of Justice,
London (1868–82)
Medievalism

Royal Crescent,
Bath, England (1767–71)
Georgian Urbanism

Royal Pavilion, Brighton,
England (1815–21)
Exoticism

Royal Saltworks, Arc-et-
Senan, France (1775–9)
Sublimism

Rusakov Club,
Moscow (1927–8)
Constructivism

S

Sacsayhuamán,
Peru (c.1475)
Pre-Columbianism

Sagrada Família Church,
Barcelona (from 1883)
Decorative Industrialism

Sainsbury Centre,
University of East Anglia,
Norwich, England (1978)
Technoism

Sainte Chapelle,
Paris (1243–8)
Gothic Scholasticism

San Andrea,
Mantua, Italy (1472–94)
Humanism

San Andrea al Quirinale,
Rome (1658–70)
Baroque

San Carlo alle Quattro
Fontane, Rome (1633–67)
Baroque

San Cataldo Cemetery,
Modena, Italy (1980)
Neo-Rationalism

San Giacomo degli
Incurabili, Rome (1590)
Pietism

San Giovanni Battista,
Florence (1960–3)
Expressionism

San Giorgio Maggiore,
Venice (1566)
Mannerism

San Lorenzo,
Florence (1421–40)
Inventionism

San Sebastiano,
Mantua, Italy (1459)
Humanism

San Stefano Rotondo,
Rome (AD 468–83)
Christian Classicism

Santa Maria della Pace,
west front and piazza,
Rome (1656–7)
Baroque

Santa Maria delle Carceri,
Prato, Italy (1485)
Idealism

Santa Maria delle Grazie,
Milan (1492–7)
Humanism

Santa Maria Novella,
Florence, facade (1456–70)
Humanism

Sant Ivo della Sapienza,
Rome (1642–60)
Baroque

Schaulager Foundation,
Basle, Switzerland (2003)
Metarationalism

School at Morbio
Inferiore, Switzerland
(1972–07)
Neo-Rationalism

School of Surgery,
Paris (1769–75)
Neoclassicism

Schroder House, Utrecht,
the Netherlands (1924–25)
Rationalism

Schullin Jewellery Shop,
Vienna (1972–4)
Postmodernism

Science Centre,
Wolfsburg, Germany
(2005)
Deconstructivism

Seagram Building,
New York (1954–8)
Skyscraperism

Secession Building,
Vienna (1898)
Decorative Industrialism

Secretariat Buildings,
New Delhi (1912–30)
Imperialism

Segesta Temple,
Sicily (424–416 BC)
Hellenic Classicism

Segesta Theatre,
Sicily (3rd century BC)
Hellenic Classicism

Seinäjoki Town Hall,
Finland (1958–60)
Functionalism

Sezincote, Gloucestershire,
England (1803–15)
Exoticism

Sheldonian Theatre,
Oxford, England (1664–9)
Anglican Empiricism

Shinto Shrine of Kamiji-
Yama, Ise, Japan (AD 701)
Shintoism

Sir John Soane's Museum,
Breakfast Parlour,
London (1812)
Sublimism

Sky House, Tokyo (1959)
Metabolism

Sony Tower, Osaka,
Japan (1976)
Metabolism

South Pagoda, Fang-
Shan, Hopei, China (AD 117)
Confucianism

The Sphinx,
Giza, Egypt (c. 2600 BC)
Pre-Classicism

Staatsgalerie, Stuttgart,
Germany (1977–84)
Postmodernism

State Pensions Office,
Prague (1929–33)
Purism

St Augustine's, Ramsgate,
England (1846–51)
Medievalism

St Basil's Cathedral,
Moscow (1555–60)
Christian Classicism

St Jean de Montmartre,
Paris (1897–1905)
Structural Rationalism

St Mark's Basilica,
Venice (1063–85)
Christian Classicism

Stockley Park,
London (1990)
Ecoism

Stourhead, Wiltshire,
England (1721–4)
Palladianism

St Pancras Station,
London (1863–5)
Victorianism

St Paul's Church,
Covent Garden, London
(1631–33)
Georgian Urbanism

St Peter's Dome,
Rome (1547–90)
Mannerism

St Sergius and St Bachus,
Istanbul (AD 525–30)
Christian Classicism

St Stephen Walbrook,
London (1672–87)
Anglican Empiricism

Student Residence,
East Anglia University,
Norwich, England (1991)
Ecoism

Sugden House,
Watford, England (1955–6)
Brutalism

Superga Temple,
Turin (1715–27)
Baroque

Swiss Re Tower (the
'Gherkin'), London (2004)
Ecoism

Sydney Opera House,
Sydney (1956–73)
Expressionism

T

Taj Mahal, Agra, India
(1630–53)
Indism

Tanjavur Temple, India
(9th–13th centuries)
Indo-Khmerism

Tempietto,
Rome (1502–10)
Humanism

Temple of Heaven,
Beijing (1420)
Confucianism

Temple of Luxor,
Egypt (1408–1300 BC)
Pre-Classicism

The Thesion
(Hephaestion),
Athens (449–444 BC)
Hellenic Classicism

Tikal temples,
Guatemala (c. AD 500)
Pre-Columbianism

Tods Store, Tokyo (2004)
Metarationalism

Tokyo City Hall,
Tokyo (1991)
Metabolism

Torre Velasca,
Milan (1954–8)
Regionalism

Trafalgar Square,
London (1840)
Monumental Urbanism

Treasury of Atreus,
Mycenae, Greece
(c.1300–1200 BC)
Proto-Classicism

TWA Terminal, JFK
Airport, New York
(1958–62)
Expressionism

U

Union Buildings, Pretoria,
South Africa (1909–12)
Imperialism

Unity Temple, Oak Park,
Chicago (1905–7)
Functionalism

University of Virginia,
Charlottesville, Virginia
(1817–26)
Neoclassicism

V

Vanna Venturi House,
Chestnut Hill, Philadelphia
(1964)
Postmodernism

Vaux le Vicomte Chateau,
Maincy, France (1657–61)
Absolutism

Versailles, Chateau de,
Paris (1661–78)
Absolutism

Vicenza Basilica,
Vicenza, Italy (1546–9)
Mannerism

Viceroy's House,
New Delhi (1912–30)
Imperialism

Victoria Memorial,
Calcutta, India (1901–21)
Imperialism

Vierzehnheiligen, Bavaria,
Germany (1743–72)
Rococo

Villa Savoye,
Poissy, France (1929–31)
Purism

Villa Seurat, Paris (1925–6)
Purism

Vitra Fire Station, Weil-
am-Rhein, Germany (1994)
Deconstructivism

Vittorio Emmanuele II
monument, Rome
(1885–1911)
Monumental Urbanism

W

Waldbuhl House, Uzwil,
Switzerland (1907–11)
Anti-Urbanism

Weissenhofseidlung
Houses, Stuttgart,
Germany (1927)
Rationalism

Wexner Center,
University of Ohio,
Athens, Ohio (1990)
Deconstructivism

Winter Palace,
St Petersburg, Russia
(1754–62)
Absolutism

Y

Yale University Art and
Architecture Building
(1958–64)
Brutalism

Yale University Art
Gallery, New Haven,
Connecticut (1951–4)
Usonianism

Yokohama Ferry
Terminal, Japan (2002)
Metarationalism

Z

Ziggurat and Precinct of
Ur, Mesopotamia
(rebuilt 2125 BC)

Zwinger Palace, Dresden,
Germany (1711–22)
Rococo

Glossary of Architects

A

AALTO, Alvar (1898–1976)
Functionalism

ADELCRANTZ, Carl Fredrik
(1716–96)
Exoticism

ADAM, Robert (1728–92)
Georgian Urbanism

AGHA, Sedefkar Mehmet
(1550–1682)
Islamicism

ALBERTI, Leon Battista
(1404–72)
Humanism

B

BAILLIE SCOTT, Mackay
Hugh (1865–1945)
Anti-Urbanism

BAKEMA, Jacob (1914–81)
Structuralism

BAKER, Herber
(1862–1946)
Imperialism

BARRAGÀN, Luis
(1902–88)
Regionalism

BARRY, Charles
(1795–1860)
Victorianism; Monumental
Urbanism

BATES, Don (1953–)
Metarationalism

BAWA, Geoffrey
(1919–2003)
Regionalism

BAUTISTA, Francisco
(1594–1679)
Pietism

BEHNISCH, Günter (1922–)
Expressionism;
Deconstructivism

BEHRENS, Peter
(1868–1940)
Decorative Industrialism;
Expressionism

BERLAGE, Hendrick
(1856–1934)
Structural Rationalism

BERNINI, Gianlorenzo
(1598–1680)
Baroque

BOFFRAND, Germain
(1667–1754)
Rococo

BORROMINI, Francesco
(1599–1667)
Baroque

BOTTA, Mario (1943–)
Neo-Rationalism

BOULLÉE, Etienne-Louis
(1728–99)
Sublimism

BRAMANTE, Donato
(1444–1514)
Humanism

BRUNEL, Isambard
Kingdom (1806–59)
Materialism

BRUNELLESCHI, Filippo
(1377–1446)
Inventionism

BUCKMINSTER FULLER,
Richard (1895–1983)
Technoism

BUON, Giovanni and
Bartolomeo
Gothic Commercialism

BURGES, William
(1827–81)
Medievalism

BURLINGTON, Lord
(1694–1753)
Palladianism

BURNHAM, Daniel
(1846–1912)
Monumental Urbanism;
Skyscraperism

BURTON, Decimus
(1800–81)
Materialism

BUTTERFIELD, William
(1814–1900)
Medievalism; Victorianism

C

CAMPBELL, Colen
(1673–1729)
Palladianism

CANDILIS, Georges
(1913–95)
Structuralism

CHALGRIN, Jean-François
Thérèse (1739–1811)
Monumental Urbanism

CHAMBERS, William
(1723–96)
Exoticism

CHISHOLM, Robert
(1840–1915)
Imperialism

COCKERELL, Samuel Pepys
(1754–1827)
Exoticism

COOK, Peter (1936–)
Technoism

CORREA, Charles (1930–)
Regionalism

CRONSTEDT, Carl Johan
(1709–77)
Exoticism

CULLINAN, Edward
(1933–)
Ecoism

D

DA BIBIENA, Giuseppe
Galli (1696–1757)
Rococo

DA CORTONA, Domenico
(1495–1549)
Regional Classicism

DA CORTONA, Pietro
(1596–1669)
Baroque

DANCE, George (Elder)
(1695–1768)
Georgian Urbanism

DANCE, George (Younger)
(1741–1825)
Georgian Urbanism;
Sublimism

DA SANGALLO, Antonio
(Elder and Younger:
1455–1534, 1485–1546)
Idealism

DA SANGALLO, Giuliano
(1445–1516)
Idealism

DAVIDSON, Peter (1955–)
Metarationalism

DA VINCI, Leonardo
(1452–1519)
Inventionism

DE ARCINIEGA, Claudio
(1527–93)
Pietism

DE BAUDOT, Anatole
(1836–1915)
Structural Rationalism

DE HERRARA, Juan
(1530–97)
Pietism

DE KLERK, Michel
(1884–1923)
Expressionism

DE LA VALLEE, Simon
(1590–1642)
Regional Classicism

DE L'ORME, Philibert
(1510–70)
Regional Classicism

DELLA PORTA, Giacomo
(1537–1602)
Pietism

DE MEURON, Pierre (1950)
Metarationalism

DE TOLEDO, Juan Bautista
(d.1567)
Pietism

DE VRIES, Nathalie (1965–)
Metarationalism

DI BARTOLOMMEO,
Michelozzo (1396–1472)
Inventionism

DIENTZENHOFER, Johann
(1689–1751)
Rococo

DURAND, Jean Nicolas
Louis (1760–1834)
Structural Rationalism

E

EAMES, Charles (1907–78)
Technoism

EAMES, Ray (1912–88)
Technoism

EISENMAN, Peter (1932–)
Deconstructivism

ELLIS, Peter (1804–84)
Materialism

EMERSON, William
(1843–1921)
Imperialism

ENSHU, Kobori
(1579–1647)
Shintoism

ERSKINE, Ralph (1913–95)
Structuralism

EVELYN, John (1620–1706)
Anglican Empiricism

F

FARRELL, Terry (1938–)
Postmodernism

FATHY, Hassan (1900–89)
Regionalism

FILARETE, Antonio
(c. 1400–69)
Idealism

FISCHER, Johann Michael
(1692–1766)
Rococo

FLITCROFT, Henry
(1697–1769)
Palladianism

FONTANA, Domenico
(1543–1607)
Pietism

FOSTER, Norman (1935–)
Technoism; Ecoism

G

GABRIEL, Jacques-Ange
(1698–1782)
Absolutism

GARNIER, Charles
(1825–98)
Monumental Urbanism

GAUDÍ, Antonio
(1852–1926)
Decorative Industrialism

GEHRY, Frank (1929–)
Deconstructivism

GHIBERTI, Lorenzo
(1378–1455)
Inventionism

GIBBS, James (1682–1754)
Anglican Empiricism

GOFF, Bruce (1904–82)
Usonianism; Regionalism

GONDOIN, Jacques
(1737–1818)
Neoclassicism

GOWAN, James (1923–)
Functionalism; Brutalism

GRAVES, Michael (1934–)
Postmodernism

GREENE, Charles
(1868–1957)
Usonianism

GREENE, Henry
(1870–1954)
Usonianism

GRIMSHAW, Nicholas
(1938–)
Technoism

GROPIUS, Walter
(1883–1969)
Rationalism

GUARINI, Guarino
(1624–83)
Baroque

GUIMARD, Hector
(1867–1942)
Decorative Industrialism

H

HADID, Zaha (1950–)
Deconstructivism

HÄRING, Hugo
(1882–1958)
Functionalism

HARRISON, Wallace
(1895–1981)
Skyscraperism

HAUSSMANN, Eugene
(1809–91)
Monumental Urbanism

HAVLÍCEK, Josef
(1899–1961)
Purism

HAWKSMOOR, Nicholas
(1661–1736)
Anglican Empiricism

HERRON, Ron (1930–94)
Technoism

HERTZBERGER, Herman
(1932–)
Structuralism

HERZOG, Jacques (1950)
Metarationalism

HOBAN, James
(1732–1831)
Neoclassicism

HOFFMANN, Josef
(1870–1956)
Decorative Industrialism

HOLL, Steven (1947–)
Metarationalism

HOLLAND, Henry
(1745–1806)
Palladianism

HOLLEIN, Hans (1934–)
Postmodernism

HONZIK, Karel (1900–66)
Purism

HOOD, Raymond
(1881–1934)
Skyscraperism

HOPKINS, Michael (1935–)
Technoism; Ecoism

HORTA, Victor (1861–1947)
Decorative Industrialism

I

IOFAN, Boris (1891–1976)
Totalitarianism

ISOZAKI, Arato (1931–)
Metabolism;
Postmodernism

ITO, Toyo (1941–)
Metarationalism

J

JACOB, Swinton
(1841–1917)
Imperialism

JEFFERSON, Thomas
(1743–1826)
Palladianism; Neoclassicism

JENNEY, William Le Baron
(1832–1907)
Skyscraperism

JOHNSON, Philip
(1906–2005)
Corporatism; Rationalism

JONES, Inigo (1573–1652)
Georgian Urbanism

JOSIC, Alexis (1921–)
Structuralism

JUVARRA, Filippo
(1678–1736)
Baroque

K

KAHN, Albert (1869–1942)
Usonianism; Corporatism

KAHN, Louis (1901–74)
Usonianism; Brutalism

KENT, William (1685–1748)
Palladianism

KIKUTAKE, Kiyonori
(1928–)
Metabolism

KOOLHAAS, Rem (1944–)
Metarationalism

KRIER, Leon (1946–)
Postmodernism

KUROKAWA, Kisho
(1934–)
Metabolism

L

LABROUSTE, Henri
(1801–75)
Structural Rationalism

LATROBE, Benjamin
(1764–1820)
Neoclassicism

LAUGIER, Marc-Antoine
(1713–69)
Neoclassicism

LAURANA, Luciano
(1420–79)
Humanism

LE CORBUSIER
(1887–1965)
Purism; Rationalism;
Brutalism; Metabolism

LEDOUX, Claude-Nicolas
(1736–1806)
Sublimism

LEONIDOV, Ivan
(1902–59)
Constructivism

LESCAZE, William
(1896–1969)
Usonianism

LETHABY, William
(1857–1931)
Decorative Industrialism

LE VAU, Louis (1612–70)
Absolutism

LEVERTON, Thomas
(1743–1824)
Georgian Urbanism

LIBESKIND, Daniel (1946–)
Metarationalism

LONGHENA, Baldassare
(1598–1682)
Baroque

LUBETKIN, Berthold
(1901–90)
Purism

LURÇAT, Andre
(1894–1970)
Purism

LUTYENS, Edwin
(1869–1944)
Anti-Urbanism; Imperialism

M

MAAS, Winy (1959–)
Metarationalism

MAKI, Fumihiko (1928–)
Metabolism

MANSART, Francois
(1598–1666)
Regional Classicism

MANT, Charles (1839–81)
Imperialism

MATHER, Rick (1937–)
Ecoism

MAY, Ernst (1886–1970)
Rationalism

MAYBECK, Bernard
(1862–1957)
Usonianism

MELNIKOV, Konstantin
(1890–1974)
Constructivism

MENDELSOHN, Erich
(1887–1953)
Expressionism

MEYER, Hannes
(1889–1954)
Rationalism

MICHELANGELO
(1475–1564)
Mannerism

MIES VAN DER ROHE,
Ludwig (1886–1969)
Rationalism; Expressionism;
Skyscraperism; Corporatism

MICHELUCCI, Giovanni
(1891–1990)
Expressionism

MILIUTIN, Nikolai
(1889–1942)
Constructivism

MOORE, Charles
(1925–94)
Postmodernism

MOUSSAVI, Farshid
(1965–)
Metarationalism

N

NASH, John (1752–1835)
Georgian Urbanism;
Exoticism

NEUMANN, Balthasar
(1687–1753)
Rococo

NEUTRA, Richard
(1892–1970)
Usonianism

NIEMEYER, Oscar (1907–)
Regionalism

NOYES, Eliot (1910–77)
Corporatism

O

OLBRICH, Josef Maria
(1867–1908)
Decorative Industrialism

OUD, Jacobus Johannes
Pieter (1890–1963)
Rationalism

OUTRAM, John (1934–)
Postmodernism

P

PALLADIO, Andrea
(1508–80)
Mannerism

PARKER, Barry (1867–1941)
Anti-Urbanism

PAXTON, Joseph
(1801–65)
Materialism

PEARSON, John
Loughborough (1817–97)
Medievalism

PELLI, Cesar (1926–)
Skyscraperism

PERRAULT, Claude
(1613–88)
Absolutism

PERRET, August
(1874–1954)
Structural Rationalism

PERUZZI, Baldassare
(1481–1536)
Mannerism

PIACENTINI, Marcello
(1881–1960)
Totalitarianism

PIANO, Renzo (1937–)
Technoism; Ecoism

POELART, Joseph
(1817–79)
Monumental Urbanism

POELZIG, Hans
(1869–1936)
Expressionism

PÖPPELMANN, Mathaüs
(1662–1736)
Rococo

PRANDTAUER, Jakob
(1660–1726)
Rococo

PRICE, Cedric (1934–2003)
Technoism

PRIX, Wolf (1942–)
Deconstructivism

PUGIN, Augustus
(1812–52)
Structural Rationalism;
Medievalism; Materialism;
Victorianism

R

RAINALDI, Carlo (1611–91)
Baroque

RASTRELLI, Bartolomeo
(1700–71)
Absolutism

REWAL, Raj (1934–)
Regionalism

RIETVELD, Gerrit
(1888–1964)
Rationalism

RITCHIE, Ian (1947–)
Ecoism

ROGERS, Ernesto
(1909–69)
Regionalism; Totalitarianism

ROGERS, Richard (1933–)
Technoism

ROMANO, Giulio
(1499–1546)
Mannerism

ROSSELLINO, Bernardo
(1409–64)
Idealism

ROSSI, Aldo (1931–97)
Neo-Rationalism

RUDOLPH, Paul (1918–97)
Brutalism

RUDNEV, Lev (1885–1956)
Totalitarianism

S

SAARINEN, Eero (1910–61)
Expressionism; Corporatism

SACCONI, Giuseppe
(1853–1905)
Monumental Urbanism

SALVIN, Anthony
(1799–1881)
Victorianism

SANMICHELI, Michele
(1484–1559)
Mannerism

SANSOVINO, Jacopo
(1486–1570)
Mannerism

SCHAROUN, Hans
(1893–1972)
Functionalism

SCHINDLER, Rudolph
(1887–1953)
Usonianism

SCHINKEL, Karl Friedrich
(1780–1841)
Neoclassicism

SCOTT, George Gilbert
(1811–77)
Victorianism

SCOTT BROWN, Denise
(1931–)
Postmodernism

SEMPER, Gottfried
(1803–79)
Structural Rationalism;
Monumental Urbanism

SERLIO, Sebastiano
(1475–1554)
Regional Classicism

SHAW, Norman
(1831–1912)
Anti-Urbanism

SHCHUSEV, Alexei
(1873–1949)
Totalitarianism

SIZA, Alvaro (1933–)
Neo-Rationalism

SKIDMORE, OWINGS &
MERRILL
Corporatism

SMIRKE, Robert
(1781–1867)
Neoclassicism

SMIRKE, Sydney
(1798–1877)
Materialism

SMITHSON, Alison
(1928–93)
Brutalism

SMITHSON, John (d. 1630)
Regional Classicism

SMITHSON, Peter
(1923–2003)
Brutalism

SMITHSON, Robert
(c. 1536–1614)
Regional Classicism

SOANE, John (1753–1837)
Sublimism

SOUFFLOT, Jacques-
Germain (1713–80)
Neoclassicism

SPEER, Albert (1904–81)
Totalitarianism

STIRLING, James
(1924–92)
Functionalism; Brutalism;
Postmodernism

STREET, George Edmund
(1824–81)
Medievalism

STUBBINS, Hugh (1912–)
Skyscraperism; Corporatism

SULLIVAN, Louis
(1856–1924)
Decorative Industrialism;
Functionalism; Usonianism;
Corporatism

SWICZINSKY, Helmut
(1944–)
Deconstructivism

T

TANGE, Kenzo
(1913–2005)
Metabolism

TATLIN, Vladimir
(1885–1953)
Constructivism

TAUT, Bruno (1880–1938)
Expressionism

TERRAGNI, Giuseppe
(1904–43)
Totalitarianism

THORPE, John
(1565–1655)
Regional Classicism

TROOST, Paul (1879–1934)
Totalitarianism

TSCHUMI, Bernard (1944–)
Deconstructivism

U

UNGERS, Oswald (1926–)
Neo-Rationalism

UNWIN, Raymond
(1863–1940)
Anti-Urbanism

UTZON, Jørn (1918–)
Expressionism

V

VAN ALEN, William
(1883–1954)
Skyscraperism

VANBRUGH, John
(1664–1726)
Anglican Empiricism

VAN CAMPEN, Jacob
(1595–1657)
Regional Classicism

VAN DE VELDE, Henri
(1863–1957)
Decorative Industrialism

VAN EYCK, Aldo (1918–99)
Structuralism

VAN RIJS, Jacob (1964–)
Metarationalism

VANVITELLI, Luigi
(1700–73)
Absolutism

VENTURI, Robert (1925–)
Postmodernism

VESNIN, Alexander
(1883–1959)
Constructivism

VIGNOLA, Jacopo
(1507–73)
Pietism

VIGNON, Pierre
(1762–1828)
Neoclassicism

VIOLLET-LE-DUC, Eugène
(1814–79)
Structural Rationalism;
Medievalism

VON ERLACH, Johann
Fischer (1656–1723)
Absolutism

VON HILDEBRANDT,
Lukas (1668–1745)
Rococo

VON KLENZE, Leo
(1784–1864)
Neoclassicism

VOYSEY, Charles Francis
Annesley (1857–1941)
Anti-Urbanism

W

WAGNER, Otto
(1841–1918)
Decorative Industrialism

WATERHOUSE, Alfred
(1830–1905)
Victorianism

WEBB, Philip (1831–1915)
Anti-Urbanism

WILKINS, William
(1778–1839)
Neoclassicism

WOOD, John (Elder)
(1704–54)
Georgian Urbanism

WOOD, John (Younger)
(1728–81)
Georgian Urbanism

WOODS, Shadrach
(1923–73)
Structuralism

WOODWARD, Benjamin
(1816–61)
Materialism

WREN (1632–1723)
Anglican Empiricism

WRIGHT, Frank Lloyd
(1867–1959)
Anti-Urbanism; Usonianism;
Corporatism

WYATT, James (1747–1813)
Exoticism

WYATT, Matthew Digby
(1820–77)
Materialism

Z

ZAERA-POLO, Alejandro
(1963–)
Metarationalism

AEDICULE
Literally 'small house', generally a smaller space defined by columns and roof within a larger space.

AISLE
A lower space divided from a higher one by a row of columns or pillars. Typically, a church has a central nave with an aisle on either side.

ARCADE
Originally a space defined by a row of arches, it has come to mean a pedestrianised and covered passage of shops.

ARCH
One of the fundamental building forms, an arch can be rounded or pointed (that is, made up of curves that are not continuous). The great strength of such shapes allows them to span openings.

ARCHITECT
The meaning of this term has changed throughout history. The first recorded architect was the Egyptian high priest Imhotep, who first used stone as a building material and was later deified. In the Middle Ages, 'architect' generally referred to God, the designer of the Universe. Now, in the industrialised world, it means someone who has completed a prescribed course of study and professional experience, though some still hark back to the earlier meanings.

ARCHITRAVE
Frame around a door or window that often covers up the rough edges at a junction.

ARTS AND CRAFTS
Term applied to a group of mainly British architects in the late 19th and early 20th centuries who followed the ideas of William Morris and, at a greater distance, John Ruskin, who considered that quality in art derived from skill and pleasure in craft.

ATRIUM
Originally the Latin word for a walled courtyard (within another building) open to the sky. Has latterly come to mean a glass-roofed multi-level internal space within a building such as an office or hotel.

AXIS
Literally a straight line, applied in architecture and town planning to long, straight routes between rooms or buildings. Often associated with expressions of power in the relationships between institutions and their occupiers.

AXONOMETRIC
A means of drawn projection, especially useful for showing volumes and popular among Modernist architects. It is based on the plan turned through 45 degrees, with vertical lines drawn upwards. As it lacks perspective the effect can appear distorting.

BALLUSTER
A pillar or post supporting a coping or handrail to serve as a barrier at a change of level, typically on a staircase or elevated terrace.

BARREL VAULT
A roof formed on the principle of an arch, but extended continuously to make a semi-circular volume.

BASILICA
Originally a large meeting or administrative hall in Roman buildings. The form was taken over by Christians as the model for churches. A typical basilica is oblong and divided lengthways into three strips. The central one (nave) is usually higher and wider than the outer pair.

BOTH-AND
Term coined by Robert Venturi to describe pluralism and heterogeneity against what he saw as the 'either-or' of simplistic Modernism.

BRISE SOLEIL
Sun-shading, often of sculpted concrete forms. Commonly a functional justification for decorative devices on the exterior of Modernist buildings.

BUTTRESS
A masonry pier projecting from a wall to give it extra strength.

CABLE NET
A lightweight roof structure capable of enclosing large spaces economically. A net of cables is pre-stressed to make it deform to the most efficient shape, calculated by computer.

CANTILEVER
A horizontal projection fixed at one end only.

CAPITAL
The top part of a column, generally wider than the shaft and often decorated.

CIAM
Congrès Internationale d'Architecture Moderne, a body formed after a conference at La Sarraz, Switzerland, in 1928. It sought to define Modernist orthodoxy largely on the lines set out by Le Corbusier and its secretary, Sigfried Giedion, until it was challenged by Team X in the 1950s.

CLADDING
Strictly a panel or sheet external wall surface that has no structural strength and so is fixed to a structural wall or frame. This approach can be found in vernacular architecture but became particularly common in frame construction from the late 19th century onwards.

CLERESTORY
High-level windows in a wall, often used in churches or law courts where views out might be thought inappropriate.

CLIENT
Person or body who commissions and generally assumes financial responsibility for construction costs, though may expect to recoup or make a profit from the outlay.

CLOISTER
A covered space looking inwards to an enclosed garden or courtyard. Often associated with privacy or contemplation, for example in monasteries.

COLONNADE
A row of columns supporting a wall, an entablature or arches.

CORBEL
A piece of stone that projects from a wall to support beams or a roof structure above. A series of corbels can form a portal that in some forms of construction substitutes for a true arch.

CORNICE
The crowning projection at the top of a Classical building. A notable feature of Florentine Renaissance palaces.

CROSSING
The junction of the nave and transepts in a church.

CUPOLA
Italian for dome. Often used for any dome on an Italian building, but in English generally refers to a small example.

CURTAIN WALL
A non-structural wall, supported by a frame, composed of solid or glazed panels.

DOME
A structural form based on curved geometry. The curves can be continuous or broken into segments, but have an inherent strength that allows large spans.

EMERGENCE TECHNOLOGY
Level of sophistication reached in IT where various outcomes can be generated from the same basic parameters.

ENTABLATURE
The part of a Classical building above the columns and below the roof, which carries much of the building's decorative potential.

ENTASIS
The swelling of a Classical column, typically reaching its maximum about one-third of its way up the height, which corrects the optical illusions that arise from vertical edges.

FACADE
An external face of a building.

FLUTING
The shallow, curving recesses cut into a column or pilaster that create patterns of shade and other optical effects.

FOOTPRINT
The area and shape a building occupies on the ground, irrespective of the height or shape of upper floors.

FOYER
Building entrance that can have an important architectural and social function in a large public institution.

FRAME
A structural skeleton, traditionally in wood, but which in steel or concrete can support much larger buildings.

GABLE
The triangular part of a roof defined by two sloping planes.

GLAZING
A wall or part of a wall of a building predominantly of glass.

GOLDEN SECTION
One of the most common proportional relationships (1:1:618) used in Classical architecture and other movements that sought authority from mathematics. Once thought to have divine or mystical properties that few architects would now recognise, but undeniably a tool in creating elegant proportions.

ICON
Strictly an image intended to inspire religious devotion, but loosely applied to buildings where exuberant or extrovert design often takes precedent over function, programme and context to create a memorable or shocking impact.

IDEAL CITY
An important idea in Renaissance architecture. The belief that well-ordered and harmonious architecture could reflect the good-ordering and harmony of the cosmos, and the divinely ordained structure of human society.

ISOMETRIC
A form of drawn projection, based on a plan but distorted to avoid the apparent discrepancies of an axonometric.

IT
Information technology has taken an increasingly large role in building design due to the realism with which unbuilt designs can be depicted and developed, and because of the rapidity

with which different structural forms can be calculated.

JUNK SPACE
Coined by Rem Koolhaas to describe the undifferentiated space of large urban buildings such as shopping centres and exhibition halls.

MEZZANINE
An intermediate floor, often smaller in area and overlooking the floor below.

MODERNISM
Unquestionably the dominant movement in the arts, including architecture, since the early 20th century, but notoriously difficult to define. A common theme of its various, often contradictory movements, is the overthrow of artistic and cultural conventions and the institution of permanent reassessment of the goals, content and purpose of art.

NAVE
The space in a church between the main entrance (often at the west end) and the crossing. Often flanked by lower aisles.

OCCUPIER
Person who uses a building, who may have had little or nothing to do with its design and commissioning, and may or may not be responsible for its management and upkeep.

ORDERS
The Orders are the fundamental element of Classical architecture and the repository of its intellectual culture. Each of the three principal Orders – Doric, Ionic and Corinthian – has its own rules that govern proportions and decorative elements.

ORTHOGONAL DRAWINGS
Drawings strictly in two dimensions that show a slice

through a building, either vertical (section or elevation) or horizontal (plan). They became the norm during the Renaissance and are a vital part of the way architects communicate instructions to builders. Devices such as shadow casting are used to show relief.

PANEL
Part of a wall finish, typically a non-load-bearing repeated modular component, which fits into a curtain-wall system and is supported on a frame.

PARAPET
Part of wall that reaches above the roof gutter to conceal both gutter and roof.

PEDIMENT
The gable end of a Classical building. Often the setting for sculptural figures.

PERISTYLE
A range of columns around a courtyard or building such as a temple.

PIANO NOBILE
Literally the noble floor, hence the principal floor of a Classical building above the base and below the attic or roof.

PIAZZA
An open-air public space in a city, often associated with a church or major civic institution.

PICTURESQUE
Literally, in the manner of a picture, but given a specific meaning in late-18th-century Britain, referring to the potential of untamed nature to evoke the sensation of the sublime.

PIER
A massive vertical structural element, often carrying a substantial load, such as elaborate vaulting or a dome.

PILASTER
A vestigial column, but only projecting slightly, often denoted by decorative features, within a continuous wall. Used to imply Classical Order.

PILLAR
A solid column that need not comply to Classical proportion or ornament.

PILOTI
Unadorned columns with no entasis. Used in Modernist architecture to raise a building off the ground, supposedly to let nature flow beneath it.

PODIUM
A continuous base on which the rest of the building sits.

POLYCHROMY
Literally, multicoloured. The term acquired a particular piquancy just before, and in the decades after 1800, when controversy raged as to whether the Ancient Greeks had used colour on their buildings.

PORTICO
A space defined by one or more rows of columns under a triangular pediment, forming a vestibule or intermediate space between exterior and interior.

PREFABRICATION
Process where elements of a building, sometimes even entire buildings or units within them, are manufactured off-site and assembled on-site. A dream of some Modernist architects for its association with industry, it did not prove wholly successful but has recently made a comeback.

PROSTYLE
A row of freestanding columns, similar to a portico.

QUADRANGLE
Four-sided courtyard. Each side may be formed by a colonnade or arcade.

RENDER
An external and supposedly waterproof external plaster.

REVIVAL
Re-use of architectural features, principles or building types in a later period, sometimes with little understanding or interest in the original circumstances that produced them. The results can be comic, tragic or even indifferent.

RUSTICATION
Bold masonry projections, often found on the base of Classical buildings, suggesting a link between the raw earth and exquisite refinement of Classical detail above.

SERVICES
Commonly, mechanical services within a building, such as heating, plumbing, ventilation, power, IT, etc.

SHELL
The basic structure and enclosure of an office building before it is fitted out to the occupier's specification. Or, a thin membrane, typically concrete, in a form that gives it structural strength so it can support itself.

SPACE TIME
A phrase coined by Sigfried Giedion, longstanding secretary of CIAM, to describe the supposed simultaneity of experience in the Modernist architecture of Le Corbusier, Walter Gropius et al, which equated Modernism with Einstein's theory of relativity and Cubist painting.

SPIRE
A tall, pointed culmination of a tower or other vertical feature.

SQUINCH
A system of arches that spring from a square plan at 45 degrees. Used to fit a polygonal tower or spire on to a square base.

STUCCO
A hard plaster commonly used to model the features of carved stonework, but considerably cheaper.

SYMBOLISM
A visual device that refers to an idea or system of ideas. Architectural decoration is often symbolic, and may refer purely to the function or programme of the building. It may also refer to a different ideological programme. Occasionally, architectural symbolism might connect the prosaic function of a building to broader cultural concepts.

TEAM X
A group of younger architects who in the 1930s first challenged and later overthrew CIAM and its prescriptive definition of Modern architecture.

TERRACOTTA
Clay-based and fired tiles or panels that can be decorative and patterned.

TORUS
An ovoid three-dimensional geometrical form, which because it is describable in mathematical terms is relatively easy to build, and so increases the buildable range of complex forms.

TRANSEPT
Projections on either side of the crossing in a church forming a minor perpendicular axis to the main axis from the west door to the altar.

USER
An innocuous-sounding word that has become problematic as buildings are increasingly commissioned by people, either for commercial or social purposes, who do not use them.

VAULT
A brick or stone arched covering to a building. Most commonly refers to Gothic architecture, where the arch is pointed rather than rounded, and formed by ribs with the space between filled in stone. Can be highly elaborate and decorative.

VERNACULAR
Indigenous architecture, using local materials and built using traditional techniques that have evolved over a long period and often have a close correlation with the social structure of the builder's society.

VOLUTE
The spiral scroll that forms the principal feature of the capital of an Ionic column. Also found in reduced form in a Corinthian column capital.

ZIGGURAT
A stepped pyramid, precursor of the Great Pyramids of Ancient Egypt. Also found in Mesopotamia and Central America.

ZONING
Now much-derided Modernist town-planning policy in which, generally for reasons of health or ideology, different functions were placed in different zones of a city. Thus, housing, industry, commerce, leisure and so on were all separated from each other.

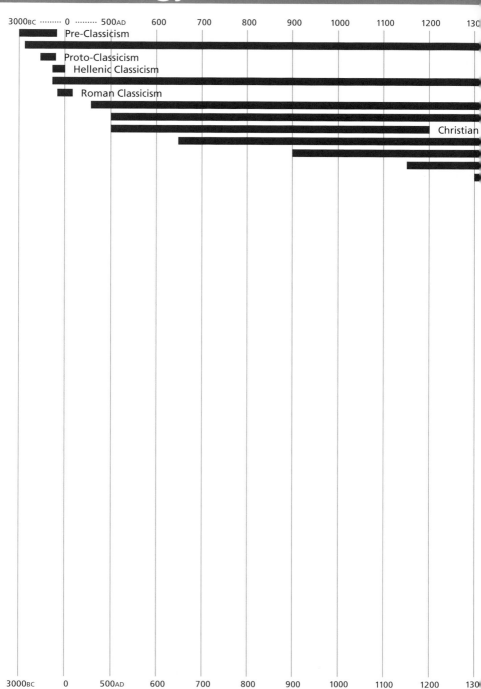

| 3000BC | ··········· 0 ·········· | 500AD | 600 | 700 | 800 | 900 | 1000 | 1100 | 1200 | 130 |

Pre-Classicism

Proto-Classicism
Hellenic Classicism

Roman Classicism

Christian

| 3000BC | 0 | 500AD | 600 | 700 | 800 | 900 | 1000 | 1100 | 1200 | 130 |

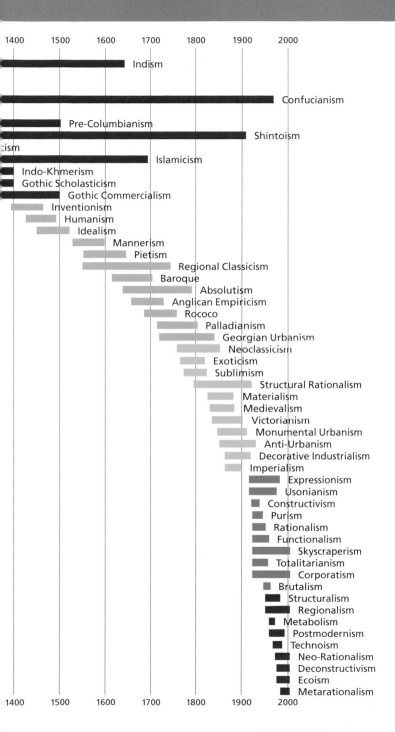

	1400	1500	1600	1700	1800	1900	2000

Indism

Confucianism

Pre-Columbianism

Shintoism

:ism

Islamicism

Indo-Khmerism

Gothic Scholasticism

Gothic Commercialism

Inventionism

Humanism

Idealism

Mannerism

Pietism

Regional Classicism

Baroque

Absolutism

Anglican Empiricism

Rococo

Palladianism

Georgian Urbanism

Neoclassicism

Exoticism

Sublimism

Structural Rationalism

Materialism

Medievalism

Victorianism

Monumental Urbanism

Anti-Urbanism

Decorative Industrialism

Imperialism

Expressionism

Usonianism

Constructivism

Purism

Rationalism

Functionalism

Skyscraperism

Totalitarianism

Corporatism

Brutalism

Structuralism

Regionalism

Metabolism

Postmodernism

Technoism

Neo-Rationalism

Deconstructivism

Ecoism

Metarationalism

1400	1500	1600	1700	1800	1900	2000

AUSTRALIA
CANBERRA Anti-Urbanism
MELBOURNE Metarationalism
SYDNEY Expressionism

AUSTRIA
VIENNA Absolutism;
Deconstructivism; Decorative
Industrialism; Monumental
Urbanism; Postmodernism; Rococo

BELGIUM
BRUSSELS Decorative Industrialism;
Monumental Urbanism

BRAZIL
RIO DE JANEIRO Regionalism

CAMBODIA
ANGKOR Indo-Khmerism

CANADA
MONTREAL Technoism

CHINA
BEIJING Confucianism
HONG KONG Skyscraperism

CZECH REPUBLIC
PRAGUE Purism

EGYPT
CAIRO Islamicism
GIZA Pre-Classicism

FINLAND
HELSINKI Functionalism

FRANCE
PARIS Absolutism;
Deconstructivism; Decorative
Industrialism; Gothic Scholasticism;
Monumental Urbanism;
Neoclassicism; Purism; Rococo;
Structural Rationalism; Sublimism;
Technoism

GERMANY
BERLIN Functionalism;
Metarationalism; Neoclassicism;
Rationalism; Structuralism;
Totalitarianism
DRESDEN Monumental Urbanism;
Rococo
MUNICH Expressionism;
Neoclassicism; Totalitarianism

GREECE
ATHENS Hellenic Classicism
CRETE Proto-Classicism

GUATEMALA
TIKAL Pre-Columbianism

INDIA
DELHI Indism; Islamicism
NEW DELHI Anti-Urbanism;
Imperialism

ISRAEL
JERUSALEM Islamicism

ITALY
FLORENCE Expressionism;
Humanism; Inventionism;
Mannerism
MILAN Humanism;
Neo-Rationalism; Regionalism;
Totalitarianism
ROME Baroque; Christian
Classicism; Humanism; Idealism;
Mannerism; Monumental
Urbanism; Pietism; Roman
Classicism; Totalitarianism
VENICE Baroque; Christian
Classicism; Gothic Commercialism;
Mannerism

JAPAN
KATSURA Shintoism
TOKYO Metabolism;
Metarationalism; Skyscraperism

MALAYSIA
KUALA LUMPUR Skyscraperism

MEXICO
MEXICO CITY Pietism; Regionalism
TEOTIHUACÁN Pre-Columbianism

THE NETHERLANDS
AMSTERDAM Expressionism;
Metarationalism; Structuralism;
Structural Rationalism
THE HAGUE Regional Classicism

NEW CALEDONIA
NOUMÉA Ecoism

PERU
CUZCO Pre-Columbianism

POLAND
WARSAW Totalitarianism

PORTUGAL
OPORTO Neo-Rationalism

REPUBLIC OF SOUTH AFRICA
PRETORIA Imperialism

RUSSIA
MOSCOW Christian Classicism;
Constructivism; Totalitarianism
ST PETERSBURG Absolutism;
Sublimism

SPAIN
BARCELONA Decorative
Industrialism; Rationalism
BILBAO Deconstructivism
CORDOBA Islamicism
MADRID Pietism

SWEDEN
DROTTNINGHOLM Exoticism
STOCKHOLM Regional Classicism

SWITZERLAND
BASLE Metarationalism

TURKEY
ISTANBUL Christian Classicism;
Islamicism

UK
CAMBRIDGE Gothic Scholasticism;
Structuralism; Technoism
EDINBURGH Georgian Urbanism
LONDON Anglican Empiricism;
Anti-Urbanism; Brutalism; Christian
Classicism; Ecoism; Exoticism;
Georgian Urbanism; Gothic
Scholasticism; Materialism;
Medievalism; Monumental
Urbanism; Neoclassicism;
Palladianism; Postmodernism;
Purism; Sublimism; Technoism;
Victorianism
OXFORD Anglican Empiricism;
Materialism; Victorianism

UKRAINE
DNEPROSTROI Constructivism

US
BALTIMORE Neoclassicism
CHICAGO Decorative
Industrialism; Functionalism;
Monumental Urbanism;
Skyscraperism; Victorianism
LOS ANGELES Technoism;
Usonianism
NEW ORLEANS Postmodernism
NEW YORK Corporatism;
Expressionism; Skyscraperism
PHILADELPHIA Postmodernism;
Usonianism
WASHINGTON Neoclassicism

Photographic Credits

First published in the United States of
America in 2006 by
UNIVERSE PUBLISHING
A Division of Rizzoli International
Publications, Inc.
300 Park Avenue South
New York, NY 10010
www.rizzoliusa.com

AN IQON BOOK

This book was designed
and produced by
Iqon Editions Limited
Sheridan House
112–116a Western Road
Hove BN3 1DD

Publisher, concept and direction:
David Breuer

Designer: Isambard Thomas

Editor and Picture Researcher:
Caroline Ellerby

Printed in Singapore by
Star Standard

ISBN-10: 0-7893-1380-4
ISBN-13: 978-0-7893-1380-5

Library of Congress Control Number
2005930004

Second printing, 2007
2007 2008 2009 2010 /
10 9 8 7 6 5 4 3 2

Cover illustration details
(left to right, from top):

The Parthenon, Athens
(pp 18–19)

Johnson Wax Headquarters, Racine,
Wisconsin (p 115)

Guggenheim Museum, Bilbao, Spain
(p 136)

Tods Store, Tokyo (p 140)

Basilica di Santa Maria del Fiore
(Florence Cathedral) (p 44)

Sydney Opera House (p 99)

The Great Pyramids, Giza, ouside Cairo
(p 13)

Centre Georges Pompidou, Paris
(pp 126–27)

Metro entrance, Porte Dauphine, Paris
(p 89)

Taj Mahal, Agra (p 15)

San Carlo alle Quattro Fontane,
Rome (p 57)

Vanna Venturi House, Chestnut Hill,
Philidelphia (p 132)

Doges Palace, Venice (p 40)

Temple 1, Tikal, Guatemala
(pp 28–29)

Keble College, Oxford University,
England (p 84)

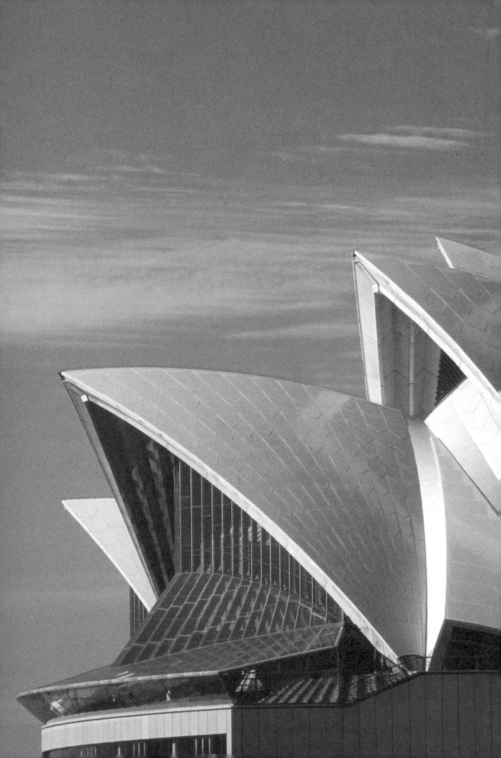